Junior Thesaurus

Cindy Leaney

Miles Kelly
PUBLISHING

Junior Thesaurus

Your thesaurus will help you to use new or different words. Each double page has a new keyword with a choice of related words called synonyms – these are words that have the same meaning as another word. Each synonym is explained and placed in an example sentence. You will also find opposites, cartoons, games and fact panels. So brighten your emails, boost your vocabulary, but most of all, have fun with words!

Keyword and synonyms

Each keyword is in large type, and is followed by a line of synonyms. Each synonym is in alphabetical order.

Laugh

burst out laughing • cackle • chortle

· to laugh in a loud way

chuckle
to laugh quietly or to yourself
I could just hear my grandad chuckling.

· to laugh in a loud way because something is funny

burst out laughing
to laugh loudly and suddenly
We looked at her and burst out laughing

guffaw
to laugh loudly in a way that is hard to control
We guffawed when she told us the joke

roar with laughter
to laugh noisily and hard
The children roared with laughter.

> The opposite of laugh is cry.

· roar with laughter

giggle
to laugh in a silly, quiet way because something is funny or you are embarrassed
We couldn't stop giggling at our teacher's tie.

A B C D E F G H I J K L

Opposites

There are small chalkboard panels throughout your book. These give the opposites of the keywords.

Alphabetical order

The words in this book are in alphabetical order. The coloured band along the bottom of every page will tell you which letter of the alphabet you are looking at.

Cartoons

These illustrate many of the words in your book in a fun way. Each cartoon has its own label to tell you exactly what it is.

Junior Thesaurus

First published in 2004 by
Miles Kelly Publishing Ltd
Bardfield Centre, Great Bardfield,
Essex, CM7 4SL

Copyright © Miles Kelly Publishing Ltd 2004
Some material in this book first appeared in *First Fun Thesaurus*

2 4 6 8 10 9 7 5 3 1

Editorial Director: Anne Marshall
Senior Editor: Belinda Gallagher
Editorial Assistant: Lisa Clayden
Designer: Louisa Leitao
Production: Estela Boulton

ISBN 1-84236-419-7

Printed in China

British Library Cataloguing-in-Publication Data
A catalogue record for this book is available from the British Library

Cartoons by Mike Foster/Maltings Partnership

www.mileskelly.net
info@mileskelly.net

Word partners

These are words that are often used together. Each word partner has an explanation and example sentence. Look for the pin boards!

Entries

Each synonym is explained and placed in an example sentence to show you how it could be used.

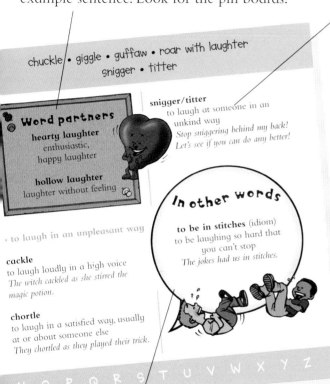

chuckle • giggle • guffaw • roar with laughter snigger • titter

Word partners

hearty laughter
enthusiastic, happy laughter

hollow laughter
laughter without feeling

snigger/titter
to laugh at someone in an unkind way
Stop sniggering behind my back!
Let's see if you can do any better!

• to laugh in an unpleasant way

cackle
to laugh loudly in a high voice
The witch cackled as she stirred the magic potion.

chortle
to laugh in a satisfied way, usually at or about someone else
They chortled as they played their trick.

In other words

to be in stitches (idiom)
to be laughing so hard that you can't stop
The jokes had us in stitches.

N O P Q R S T U V W X Y Z

In other words

An idiom is a phrasing of words that gives a different meaning from each of the words on their own. Idioms are fun ways to say things. We use them more in speech than when we are writing. Look for the speech bubbles to find more idioms.

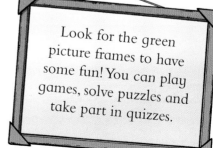

Did you know?

These panels give interesting information about words such as where they came from and how old they are.

Look for the green picture frames to have some fun! You can play games, solve puzzles and take part in quizzes.

Angry

annoyed • cross • furious • indignant

• feeling a little angry

annoyed
feeling slightly angry or impatient
Arran will be annoyed if we forget his birthday.

cross
feeling a little angry
Our teacher gets cross when we are naughty.

irritated
feeling annoyed about something that keeps happening
I'm really irritated – this game keeps crashing.

• feeling angry or very angry

furious
extremely angry
There was a furious row going on between the two teams.

irate
to feel angry because something has upset you
The Internet company received a lot of irate emails from angry customers.

livid
to feel so angry that you can't think
Angry? She was livid!

mad
feeling angry
This DVD player makes me so mad!

cross

A B C D E F G H I J K L M

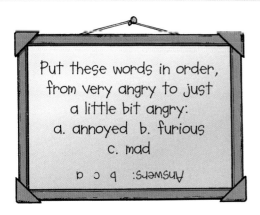

Put these words in order, from very angry to just a little bit angry:
a. annoyed b. furious
c. mad

Answers: b c a

seething
to be angry without saying a word
He was so tense, you could tell he was seething.

• **feeling upset because something is wrong or not fair**

indignant
feeling angry because something is wrong, unfair or insulting
Many parents wrote indignant letters when the playgroup closed.

resentful
feeling angry about something that is unfair and you cannot change
Some of us resent the new rules, but we all have to follow them.

In other words

to have steam coming out of your ears (idiom)
to be really angry about something
Wow! You could almost see the steam coming out of his ears!

Argue

bicker • clash • debate • dispute • feud

• to argue

bicker
an argument that isn't too serious
They bickered about who should have won the game.

clash
to fight or argue in public
The rioters clashed with police.

fight/row
to argue noisily
Why are you always fighting with your brother?

▼ squabble

quarrel
to argue with a friend or someone in your family
They quarrelled over whose turn it was to play the game.

squabble
to argue about something trivial.
Stop squabbling over those sweets!

Can you unscramble these angry words?

divli
etrai
srocs

Answers: livid irate cross

A B C D E F G H I J K L M

• **an argument**

debate
an argument where opposite views
are discussed
The debate was very heated.

dispute
an official fight between groups
or countries
The dispute was about land.

feud
a long fight between two groups
or families
Why did the family feud start?

> The opposite of
> angry is calm.

In other words

to fight like cat and dog
(idiom)
to argue all the time
*My sister and brother
fight like cat and dog.*

spat/tiff
a small argument
It was just a tiff – it will soon blow over.

Ask

consult
to ask for advice or information from an expert
Consult your doctor first.

enquire
to ask for information
Tourists can enquire at the information centre.

> ### The opposite of ask is answer.

interrogate
to ask someone a lot of questions about a crime
The police interrogated the suspect for several hours.

interview
to ask someone questions for a newspaper or TV programme, or to find out if they are right for a job
The manager interviewed everyone who applied for the job.

plead
to ask someone for something that you really want
The children pleaded with their mother for some more chocolate.

plead

poll

a study that asks a lot of people about their opinion of something
The poll shows 75 percent of people agree with the laws.

pump

to ask someone a lot of questions to get as much information as possible
We pumped them for all the information about the new campsite.

query

to ask because you have not understood something or do not think it is right
They queried the bill.

question

to ask someone a lot of questions
The headmaster questioned each pupil about who had broken the window.

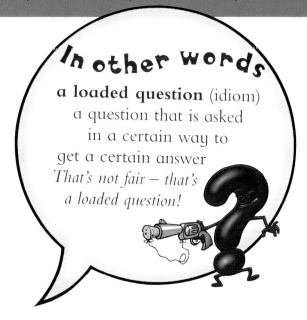

In other words

a loaded question (idiom)
a question that is asked in a certain way to get a certain answer
That's not fair – that's a loaded question!

quiz

to ask questions about something, usually in an annoying way
They quizzed us about the new teacher.

survey

to ask people a set of questions
We surveyed the school and found that most children have a mobile phone.

• something that is bad

appalling
something that seems bad in a shocking way
The prisoners' quarters were appalling.

dreadful
something that is very unpleasant or of poor quality
It was a dreadful film — don't bother to go and see it.

ghastly
something that is very unpleasant or shocking
That's a violent, ghastly game!

terrible
something that is very unpleasant or frightening
It was a terrible storm.

• bad at doing something

inept
not skilled
The inept goalkeeper let in a total of six goals.

In other words

to have a bad hair day (idiom)
a funny way to say that your hair is in a mess and everything is going wrong
I'm having a really bad hair day!

The opposite of bad is good.

hopeless/useless
to be not very good at doing something
I'm useless at maths, I can't even do simple sums.

• something that is not good quality

inferior
not as good as something or someone else
These trainers are cheaper than the more expensive brands but they're of inferior quality.

• badly behaved

mischievious
someone who causes minor annoyance or trouble
He had a very mischievious sense of humour.

naughty
badly behaved, usually to do with a child
It's very naughty to hit someone.

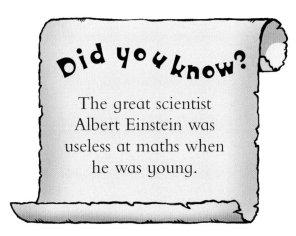

Did you know?

The great scientist Albert Einstein was useless at maths when he was young.

to say something loudly

cry
to speak in a loud voice because something is wrong
"Get a doctor!" they cried.

scream
to cry out loudly because you are excited, frightened or angry
The witch turned and all the children in the audience screamed out loud.

◀ scream

In other words

to call a spade a spade (idiom)
to tell the truth about something, even if it is not very polite
She is very direct and just calls a spade a spade.

A B C D E F G H I J K L M

shout
to speak as loud as you can
No need to shout! I can hear you!

shriek
to give a short, high cry
We all shrieked and clapped when our team won the game.

yell
to speak in a loud voice, usually because you are angry
The prisoner was yelling at the policemen outside.

• **to order someone to come to a place**

summon
to order someone to be at a certain place
I was summoned to give evidence.

• **to telephone**

phone/ring
to telephone
I'll give you a ring later.

• **to call someone or something a name**

name
to give someone a name
What are you going to name the kitten?

Can you understand this text message?

Call me L8R-K8

Answer:
Call me later – Kate

Carry

bring • fetch • haul • lift

bring

to take something to the person speaking

Bring your homework to my house and we'll work on the essay together.

fetch

to go somewhere to get something and then bring it back

Our dog is good at fetching sticks.

haul

to drag or pull something heavy

Four men hauled the box around the corner.

haul

fetch

lift

to raise something in the air

We lifted the baby out of his pram.

lug

to carry something, especially something heavy

We lugged a big bag of newspapers around all the houses.

A B C D E F G H I J K L M

support
to hold something up
They supported the stone blocks on wooden logs and rolled them along.

take
to carry something in a direction away from the person speaking
Take your jacket with you, it's going to rain.

tote
to carry something, especially something awkward or large
You can take it, but you'll have to tote it around all day.

transport
to take goods from one place to another
Brand new cars are usually transported on special lorries.

In other words

to carry the weight of the world on your shoulders
(idiom)
to feel worried or sad about things
She looks so worried – as if she has the weight of the world on her shoulders.

• **good at learning or thinking**

brainy
intelligent and good at studying
Our last teacher liked brainy kids who got all the answers right.

bright
used to talk about someone who is intelligent and clever
George is one of the brightest pupils.

▲ bright

intelligent
good at learning and understanding things
You need to be intelligent to be a doctor.

quick
able to understand things quickly
She has a quick mind.

smart
someone who is able to solve problems or who learns easily
That's a great idea! You're so smart!

• **having a lot of knowledge or information**

intellectual
educated in subjects that need to be studied for a long time
The discussion was very intellectual.

Did you know?

The word 'clever' comes from the Norwegian word *klover* – meaning ready or skilful.

The opposites of clever are foolish and unintelligent.

streetwise
experienced in living in a city
The kids in that neighbourhood are pretty streetwise.

knowledgeable
knowing a lot about a subject
The librarian is knowledgeable about a lot of things.

• **good at using your brain to get along**

cunning
able to think and plan secretly so that you get what you want
They had a very cunning plan that almost worked.

In other words

a brain box (idiom)
someone who is very intelligent
She's a bit of a brain box — she won the school quiz.

Cold

• something that is a bit cold

chilly
quite cold
Autumn is here and it's starting to get chilly at night.

cool
slightly cold
There's a nice, cool breeze down on the beach.

In other words

cool as a cucumber (idiom)
very relaxed under pressure
Dom is always as cool as a cucumber during exam time.

draughty
a draughty place has cold air blowing through it
My room is cold and draughty.

◀ draughty

A B Ç C D E F G H I J K L M

• something that is very cold

freezing
below the temperature at which water freezes
Polar bears live in freezing conditions.

The opposite of cold is hot.

frosty
extremely cold
It was a clear, frosty morning.

• a person or animal that is cold

shivering
to be so cold that you shake slightly
The puppies were wet and shivering.

to have goosepimples or goosebumps
to be so cold (or frightened) that your skin raises up in little bumps
By the end of the walk we were covered in goosepimples.

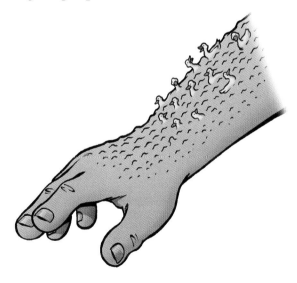

goosepimples

Different

• unlike something else

dissimilar
not the same
The twins look dissimilar.

diverse
used to talk about many things
being different from each other
The menu has very diverse dishes.

not at all like
something that is quite different
My house is not at all like yours.

• to be different from everything else

distinctive
something that is easy to recognise
because it is different
The owl has a distinctive call.

individual
a different way of doing something
She has an individual way of singing.

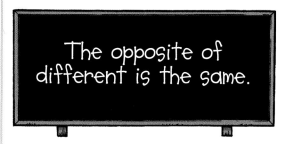

The opposite of different is the same.

unique
not like anything else
Seeing dolphins is a unique experience.

• to differ

contrast with
to be obviously different from
something else
*In contrast with the labrador, the Jack
Russell is very lively.*

A B C D E F G H I J K L M

vary
to be different from other things
in a group
*All the items of clothing vary in
size and colour.*

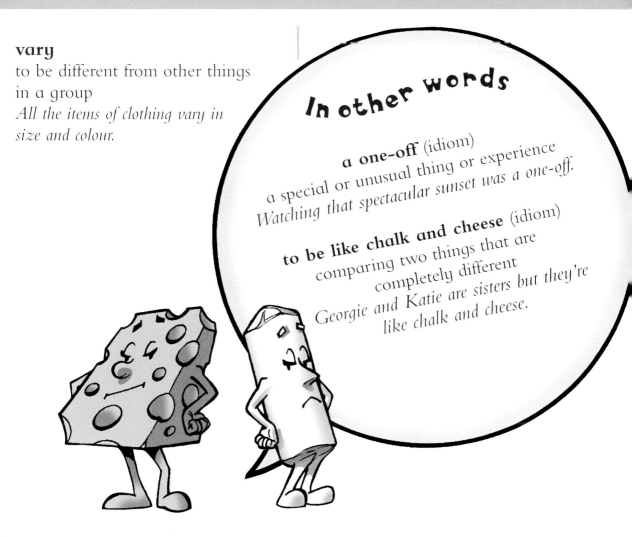

In other words

a one-off (idiom)
a special or unusual thing or experience
Watching that spectacular sunset was a one-off.

to be like chalk and cheese (idiom)
comparing two things that are
completely different
*Georgie and Katie are sisters but they're
like chalk and cheese.*

Difficult

• not easy

awkward
difficult in a way that makes people uncomfortable
My little sister is always asking awkward questions.

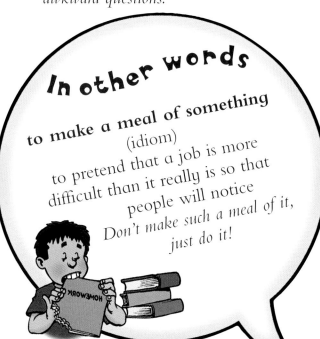

In other words

to make a meal of something
(idiom)
to pretend that a job is more difficult than it really is so that people will notice
Don't make such a meal of it, just do it!

challenging
something that is not easy but is interesting or fun to work on
Writing a page for our school website is challenging.

demanding
needing hard work or a big effort
Being at school all day can be demanding for young children.

hard
not easy to understand or do
These sums are really hard.

impossible
so difficult that it can't be done
It's impossible for me to meet you.

tough
needing a lot of thought or work
Those exams are very tough.

A B C D E F G H I K L M

**demanding • fiddly • gruelling • hard • impossible
strenuous • tough • tricky**

• not easy to do because it is complicated

fiddly
full of lots of small things or problems
This jigsaw is really fiddly.

tricky
full of problems
Decorating a birthday cake can be quite tricky.

• not easy to do because it is physically hard

backbreaking
needing a lot of physical work, especially lifting heavy things
Gardening can be backbreaking work.

gruelling
tiring and difficult because it lasts a long time
In Victorian times, children worked long, gruelling hours in factories.

strenuous
needing a lot of physical effort
Cross country skiing is a strenuous sport.

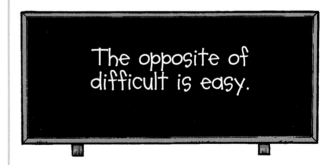

The opposite of difficult is easy.

N O P Q R S T U V W X Y Z

Drink

drain
to drink the last drop of something
Luke drained his water bottle before he got back to camp.

gulp
to drink something very quickly in large mouthfuls
I was so thirsty I gulped the juice down.

guzzle
to drink a lot of something very quickly
We guzzled our fizzy drinks.

lap up
the way animals drink with their tongues
The kittens lapped up all the milk.

Did you know?

The words 'lap', 'sip' and 'drink' all come from Old English.

polish off
to finish drinking something that you like
Hannah polished off all the apple juice.

polish off

A B C D E F G H I J K L M

quench (your thirst)

to drink something so that you stop being thirsty

We stopped halfway up the hill and quenched our thirst.

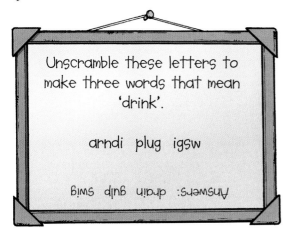

Unscramble these letters to make three words that mean 'drink'.

arndi   plug   igsw

Answers: drain gulp swig

swallow

to make something such as food or drink go down your throat

This milk tastes so sour that it's hard for me to swallow.

swallow

sip

to drink small mouthfuls of something

Just sip water slowly after you've been running.

swig

to drink something in large mouthfuls

We walked around the funfair and swigged lemonade.

• not difficult to understand or do

effortless
something that is not easy, but it is made to look easy because someone does it well
Ballet dancers make dancing look so effortless.

simple
easy to do or understand
She knew the answers so the test was simple.

The opposite of easy is difficult.

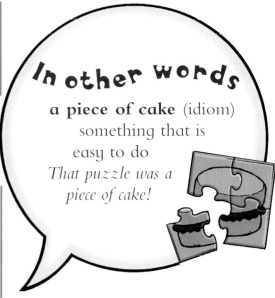

In other words

a piece of cake (idiom)
something that is easy to do
That puzzle was a piece of cake!

straightforward
easy to do because it is clear what needs to be done
Painting walls is pretty straightforward.

uncomplicated
easy to understand or to do
Games for very young children need to be uncomplicated.

• easy to do

a breeze
very easy to do
The girls were much better so beating the boys was a breeze.

a breeze

a doddle
very easy to do, especially things such as tests (informal)
The short words in the spelling test were a real doddle.

• easy to use

idiot-proof
extremely easy to use
You can buy digital cameras that are idiot-proof.

painless
not needing a lot of effort
Raising money for the school was painless.

user-friendly
clear and easy to use, especially to do with electronic things
This DVD is really user-friendly.

user-friendly

Eat

• to eat food

chew
to grind food with your teeth so that you can swallow it
This meat is hard to chew.

consume
eat
Once opened, this product should be consumed within two days.

feed
how animals eat
The panda feeds on bamboo.

munch
to eat noisily
The people behind us were munching crisps all through the film.

• to eat quickly

bolt
to eat food quickly because you are in a hurry
We bolted our lunch so we could get back to the game.

demolish
a funny way to say that someone ate all of something quickly
They demolished the food at the party within 15 minutes.

▼ munch

devour
to eat something quickly because you are very hungry
We devoured the picnic in minutes.

A B C D E F G H I J K L M

• to eat a little

In other words

could eat a horse (idiom)
very hungry
What's for dinner? I could eat a horse!

nibble
to take small bites
*Our rabbit nibbles at carrots
and lettuce.*

▼ nibble

gobble
to eat quickly
*We gobbled our breakfast as we ran to
catch the bus.*

scoff
to eat something quickly and
greedily
What! You scoffed the lot?

snack
a small meal or to eat a small meal
*We had a snack when we got home
because supper wasn't ready.*

brisk
fast and energetic
We had a brisk walk along the seafront.

quick
fast
It was a quick decision.

rapid
very fast
The team made rapid progress.

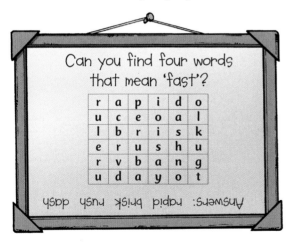

Can you find four words that mean 'fast'?

r	a	p	i	d	o
u	c	e	o	a	l
l	b	r	i	s	k
e	r	u	s	h	u
r	v	b	a	n	g
u	d	a	y	o	t

Answers: rapid brisk rush dash

speedy
fast and successful
Wishing you a speedy recovery.

The opposite of fast is slow.

• **moving fast**

quickly
fast, usually for a short time
Walk past the house as quickly.

• **to go fast**

accelerate
to go more quickly, usually in a vehicle
The driver accelerated near the finish.

quick • quickly • rapid • rush • speedy • supersonic

dash

• capable of going fast

dash
to move quickly
They dashed out of the house to try and catch the bus.

rush
to move quickly because you are in a hurry
There's no need to rush your meal!

high-speed
to move very fast
The dentist uses a high-speed drill.

supersonic
can move faster than the speed of sound
Concorde was a supersonic plane.

N O P Q R S T U V W X Y Z

Friend

amiable • buddy • circle • companion

• friend

buddy (mate/pal)
friend
We're all very good mates.

companion
someone you spend a lot of time with
They are travelling companions.

• a group of friends

circle
the people you know
We have a big circle of friends.

crowd
a group of friends you go out and do things with
A crowd of us are going out tonight, do you want to come?

In other words

china
mate
(Cockney rhyming slang)
This comes from 'china plate' which rhymes with mate.

gang
a group of friends that meet often
It's a nice gang of people.
• friendly

A B C D E **F** G H I J K L M

• friendly

amiable
friendly and likeable
He's so amiable and really easy to get along with.

hospitable
friendly and welcoming
Her parents are very hospitable and always ask us if we want something to eat or drink.

neighbourly
friendly and helpful
The new people next door are very neighbourly.

smarmy
someone who is polite and friendly but in a false way
I don't like him, he's smarmy.

sociable
friendly and out-going
Their family is very sociable, they have lots of parties.

warm
friendly and caring
Jemma is a sweet, warm girl.

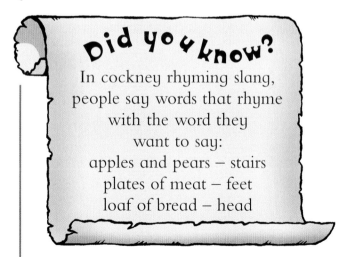

Did you know?
In cockney rhyming slang, people say words that rhyme with the word they want to say:
apples and pears – stairs
plates of meat – feet
loaf of bread – head

Frightened

afraid • chilling • dreading

• frightened

afraid
feeling nervous or frightened of something
Are you afraid of spiders?

dreading
not wanting to do something because something bad may happen
I'm really dreading the school play.

panic-stricken
so frightened that you can't think
The panic-stricken people tried to run away.

petrified
to feel so frightened that you can't even move
We were absolutely petrified.

scared
feeling worried that something bad will happen
We were so scared, we thought that someone was trying to break into the house.

terrified
very frightened of something dangerous or nasty
They were terrified of the dog and just ran without looking back.

afraid

A B C D E F G H I J K L M

- **frightening**

chilling
very frightening, sometimes in a cruel or dangerous way
It was a chilling thought.

hair-raising
frightening because something is dangerous
The story of their escape was hair-raising.

 hair-raising

In other words

scared of your own shadow (idiom)
always nervous and frightened
He's scared of his own shadow.

scary
frightening
That Hallowe'en mask is too scary.

spooky
frightening in a strange way
The castle is really spooky in the middle of the night.

N O P Q R S T U V W X Y Z

Funny

• **making you laugh**

amusing
funny and entertaining
Her stories are always amusing.

comical
funny in an unexpected way
Watching you try to catch the dog was really comical.

comical

hilarious
extremely funny
The jokes on that website are hilarious.

humorous
funny, entertaining and clever
This is a humorous book about a trip around the world.

light-hearted
funny or poking fun in a gentle way
The programme is a light-hearted look at living on a farm.

In other words

a good sense of humour
an ability to laugh and see the funny side of things
He's got a good sense of humour and is a lot of fun to be with.

A B C D E **F** G H I J K L M

witty
using words in a funny and
entertaining way
Uncle Derek is very witty.

• **a person who is funny**

clown
a person whose
job it is to act
silly and make
people laugh
*The clown at
the circus had
us all in
stitches.*

How many words can you
make from 'hilarious'?
You should be able to
make at least six.

Answers: hi our sir so as sour

comedian
a person whose job is to
make people laugh
*I want to be a comedian
when I grow up.*

◀ clown

• to give something to someone

donate
to give something to an
organization or group
We donated a computer to charity.

hand
to pass something from your
hand to another person's hand
Hand me that book, will you?

pass on
to give someone information
or papers
Thanks, I'll pass it on to the manager.

> The opposite of
> give is take.

slip
to give someone
something secretly
*She slipped me a note
as I walked past.*

slip

**• to give someone
something because of what
they've done**

award
to officially give someone a prize
*They awarded the medals after the
competition.*

present
to give someone something as part
of a ceremony
The headmaster presented the prizes.

reward
to give someone something for
being helpful
*We rewarded the person who found
our cat.*

• **to give something to a group**

distribute
to give something to a large group
The charity distributes medicine.

share out
to divide something into equal parts
and give a part to each person in
a group
*We won a bag of sweets and shared
them out among the team.*

• **to arrange to give someone
something after you die**

bequeath
to officially arrange to give
someone something after you
have died
*They bequeathed the land to the
tennis club.*

In other words

give and take (idiom)
a situation between two groups
or two people when each is allowed
some of the things they want
*Brothers and sisters
have to give
and take.*

Good

amazing • brilliant • decent • excellent

• something you like or enjoy

amazing/incredible
something that is good in a
surprising way
This DVD is amazing!

brilliant
very, very good
This website is brilliant!

In other words

as good as gold
(idiom)
well behaved
*Eliza has been as
good as gold today.*

excellent
extremely good
Their new CD is excellent.

fantastic/marvellous/wonderful
something good that makes you
feel excited
*The view from the top of the mountain
is fantastic.*

fun
enjoyable
This party game is fun.

great
very good or enjoyable
That ride is great! Let's go on it again.

lovely/nice
pleasant
*Thank you for letting us stay, we've
had a really nice time.*

A B C D E F **G** H I J K L M

fantastic • fun • great • impressive • incredible • lovely
marvellous • nice • outstanding • talented • wonderful

• something that is very well done or of high quality

impressive
something that is done to a high standard that you admire
That last goal was really impressive.

outstanding

The opposite of good is bad.

• to be able to do something well

outstanding
something that is noticeably better than others
Einstein was an outstanding scientist.

talented
to be naturally able to do something well
They made him captain of the team because he is the most talented player.

• morally good

decent
good and honest
Giving the money to charity was the decent thing to do.

N O P Q R S T U V W X Y Z

Happy

• **feeling happy**

cheerful
feeling happy most of the time
She's usually such a cheerful person to have around.

content
happy and satisfied in a quiet way
On a rainy day, I'm content sitting inside with a good book.

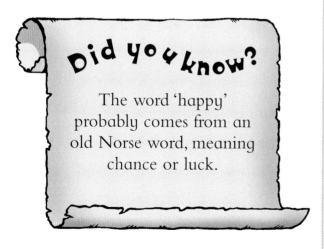

Did you know?

The word 'happy' probably comes from an old Norse word, meaning chance or luck.

jolly
happy or enjoyable
Old King Cole was a jolly old soul.

• **happy that something has happened**

delighted
very happy that something has happened
We're delighted to have won first place.

ecstatic
extremely happy and very excited that something has happened
The band was ecstatic when they won the music award.

glad
happy that something has happened or changed
I'm so glad I found my mobile phone.

In other words

over the moon (idiom)
very pleased about something
Mum got the job and she's over the moon.

overjoyed
very happy about some good news
They were overjoyed when they heard the results.

pleased
happy and satisfied that something good has happened
Our teachers were pleased with the art exhibition.

thrilled
very excited and happy
She was thrilled with the presents.

joyful
full of joy and happiness
The children were joyful that Christmas had arrived.

The opposite of happy is sad.

Hate

• to dislike or hate something

abhor
to strongly dislike or disapprove of something
They abhor violence.

despise
to strongly dislike something and think it is wrong
We despise bullying.

detest
to strongly dislike or hate something or someone
Unfairness is something that most people detest.

can't bear

loathe
to strongly dislike something
Some people loathe cabbage.

can't bear/stand
to dislike something so much that it upsets you
I can't bear scary movies!

loathe

A B C D E F G H I J K L M

• a feeling of hating something or someone

animosity
a feeling of angry hatred
There is a great deal of animosity between the two teams.

contempt
a feeling of hatred about something that you think is worthless
The school has nothing but contempt for students who are bullies.

In other words

a pet hate (idiom)
something that you don't like at all because it annoys you
Mobile phones are my teacher's pet hate.

The opposite of hate is love.

Hot

• not cold

lukewarm
only slightly warm (liquid or food)
The bathwater isn't really hot, just lukewarm.

scalding
very hot (liquid or steam)
Careful, that water is scalding!

warm
a temperature between hot and cool
Are you warm enough?

In other words

hot air (idiom)
when someone is full of hot air, they say things that they don't mean or don't really know
Their promises turned out to be so much hot air.

The opposite of hot is cold.

• hot (weather or places)

baking
very hot and dry
It's baking on the beach.

balmy
pleasantly warm
The weather is surprisingly balmy for the time of year.

boiling
very hot and uncomfortable
It's boiling in here, open a window.

muggy
hot and damp
Muggy weather makes you feel tired.

roasting
very hot and uncomfortable
I'm roasting in this sleeping bag.

roasting

sweltering

sweltering
very hot and damp
Sports day was unbearable — the weather was sweltering.

• hot (food)

spicy
tasting hot
Do you like very spicy curry?

N O P Q R S T U V W X Y Z

conceive of
to invent something, like a plan or an idea
He conceived of the idea when he was very young.

daydream
to spend time imagining nice things so that you forget about what you are doing or where you are
Stop daydreaming and pay attention!

Word partners

a vivid imagination
a powerful ability to imagine things
My older sister has a very vivid imagination.

dream of
to imagine something good that you want to happen
She's always dreamed of having a horse.

▶ fantasise

fantasise
to imagine something that probably won't happen
Mum and Dad fantasise about what they'll do when they win the lottery.

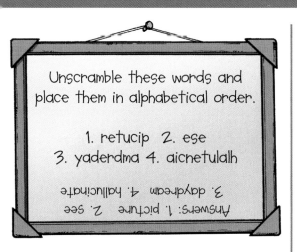

Unscramble these words and place them in alphabetical order.

1. retucip 2. ese
3. yaderdma 4. aicnetulalh

Answers: 1. picture 2. see 3. daydream 4. hallucinate

hallucinate

to believe that you can see things that aren't really there

Sometimes when you have a high fever, you hallucinate.

picture

to have a picture of something in your mind

I know who you mean but I can't picture his face.

see

to have a picture of something in your mind

I can just see you in that jacket.

visualise

to get a clear picture of something in your mind

I'm sorry, I can't visualise what you mean.

picture

N O P Q R S T U V W X Y Z

Important

central
main
Peter Pan is the central character in the play.

central

critical
extremely important to the success of something
Finishing on time is critical.

crucial
important because other things depend on it
The support of parents is crucial.

essential
important to the highest degree
It is essential that we leave work on time this evening.

historic
so important that it will cause something to be remembered as part of history
It was a historic decision.

key
important to what will happen
Hard work is a key factor to the success of the company.

The opposite of important is unimportant.

A B C D E F G H I J K L M

In other words

VIP (abbreviation)
Very Important Person
They treated us like VIPs.

significant
having an important effect
It is a significant win.

vital
very important and
necessary
Your help is vital.

weighty

major
one of the most important
Edinburgh is a major Scottish city.

notable
important and deserving attention
A notable feature of the school is the sports centre.

weighty
important and
serious
These are weighty questions.

Job
assignment • chore • duty • errand • mission

assignment
a piece of work that
someone gives you
*The assignment
is to write a
600-word essay.*

assignment

mission
an important job that
someone goes
somewhere to do
*The mission is to bring
back the secret formula.*

chore
a boring job you
have to do often
*Feeding the pets isn't really a chore,
it's fun.*

project
an important piece
of work that needs lots of
planning
This is a long-term project.

duty
something that you have a
responsibility to do
At scout camp, everyone has duties.

task
a piece of work
*Each person is given a task so that the
work gets done more quickly.*

errand
a small job
*While you're out, will you run some
errands for me?*

undertaking
a big and important job
*Raising money for a new sports hall is
a huge undertaking.*

A B C D E F G H I J K L M

• **jobs that people do to earn money**

occupation
a person's full-time job
His occupation is police officer.

profession
a job for which you need special training
He's a doctor by profession

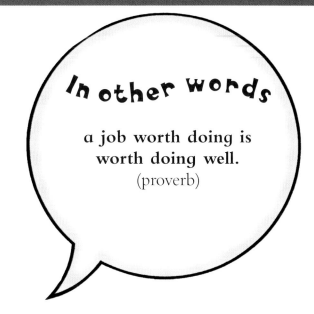

In other words

a job worth doing is worth doing well.
(proverb)

Unscramble the letters to find four words that mean 'job'.

1. ktsa   2. reoch
3. rrndea   4. uytd

Answers: 1. task 2. chore 3. errand 4. duty

trade
a skilled job that you use your hands to do
He chose carpentry as his trade.

vocation
a job that you do because you feel strongly about doing it
Teaching and nursing are vocations.

Joke

gag • in jest • practical joke • prank

▶ pun

gag
a short joke
The comedian had some good gags.

in jest
said to make people laugh
It was said in jest — he didn't really mean it!

practical joke
a carefully planned joke
My brother played a practical joke on his best friend.

prank
a silly trick that isn't supposed to hurt anyone
We played a few pranks on Hallowe'en.

pun
a play on words that sound the same but mean something else
a pun: Why was six scared of seven? Because seven eight nine!

Can you guess the answer to this joke?

What type of sandals do frogs wear?

Answer: Open-toad!

to be joking/kidding
not serious
I was only joking, I didn't really forget your birthday!

wisecrack
a funny, clever remark
He's full of wisecracks!

wisecrack

punch line
the last line of a joke that makes it funny
Mum loves to tell jokes but she always forgets the punch line.

riddle
a strange or difficult question that usually has a funny answer
Not all riddles are jokes.

In other words

to pull someone's leg (idiom)
to tell someone something that isn't true, as a joke
I think Joe was pulling your leg, there isn't a frog in the bath.

N O P Q R S T U V W X Y Z

Jump

bound
to move quickly with big jumps
Kangaroos bound across the bush.

hop
to jump on one leg
The first part of the race is hopping for 25 metres.

hurdle
to jump over something while you are running
They hurdled the fence.

leap
to jump a long way
It was a huge leap from one step to the next.

In other words

jump the gun (idiom)
do something too soon
Now, don't jump the gun. Let's just think about this a bit more.

jump to conclusions (idiom)
to decide what you think about something before you know all the facts
I'm not to blame! Why do you always jump to conclusions about me?

pounce

pounce
to jump to catch something
The cat pounced on the mouse.

skip
to go forward with small, quick jumps
We tried to skip all the way to school but we got too tired.

vault
to jump over something
The thief vaulted over the wall.

spring

spring
to jump suddenly and quickly
The cheetah seemed to spring from nowhere.

⬤ Word partners
jump at
to eagerly take the opportunity to do something
He jumped at the chance of going to the party.

N O P Q R S T U V W X Y Z

• to know something

appreciate
to understand that a situation is difficult or important
Do you appreciate how serious this situation could be?

be aware of
to know about something
Are you aware of the new rule?

be familiar with
to know about something
We're familiar with the area, we went there on holiday last year.

be well-up on
to be well-informed and up to date about a subject
He's well-up on the dates of all the important football fixtures.

feel
to know something through your feelings
You could feel the tension in the room.

realise
to notice or understand something that you didn't before
I didn't realise it was so late.

feel

sense
to have the strong feeling that you know something even though there is no proof
They sensed something was in the room.

• a person who knows about something

expert
someone who knows a lot about a certain subject
He's an expert cook.

specialist
someone who has studied a subject carefully and knows a lot about it
She's a specialist in Chinese medicine.

In other words

to know something like the back of your hand (idiom)
to know something very well
I know this wood like the back of my hand.

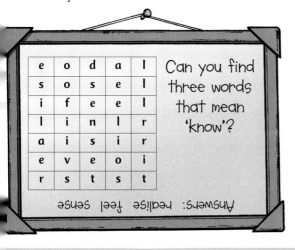

e	o	d	a	l
s	o	s	e	l
i	f	e	e	l
l	i	n	l	r
a	i	s	i	r
e	v	e	o	i
r	s	t	s	t

Can you find three words that mean 'know'?

Answers: realise feel sense

Laugh

* to laugh in a loud way

chuckle
to laugh quietly or to yourself
I could just hear my grandad chuckling.

The opposite of laugh is cry.

roar with laughter

giggle
to laugh in a silly, quiet way because something is funny or you are embarrassed
We couldn't stop giggling at our teacher's tie.

* to laugh in a loud way because something is funny

burst out laughing
to laugh loudly and suddenly
We looked at her and burst out laughing.

guffaw
to laugh loudly in a way that is hard to control
We guffawed when she told us the joke.

roar with laughter
to laugh noisily and hard
The children roared with laughter.

chuckle • giggle • guffaw • roar with laughter
snigger • titter

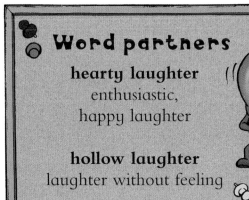

Word partners

hearty laughter
enthusiastic, happy laughter

hollow laughter
laughter without feeling

snigger/titter
to laugh at someone in an unkind way
Stop sniggering behind my back!
Let's see if you can do any better!

In other words

to be in stitches (idiom)
to be laughing so hard that you can't stop
The jokes had us in stitches.

• to laugh in an unpleasant way

cackle
to laugh loudly in a high voice
The witch cackled as she stirred the magic potion.

chortle
to laugh in a satisfied way, usually at or about someone else
They chortled as they played their trick.

N O P Q R S T U V W X Y Z

Look

• to look at or see something quickly

glance
to look at something or someone for a short time
She glanced at her watch.

glimpse
to see someone or something for a very short time
We just glimpsed some baby birds.

• to notice or see something

 peep

spot
to see or notice something or someone
We spotted several people who were wearing the same costume.

spy
to see or notice something or someone, usually from a distance
We spied them coming up the street.

• to look at someone or something secretly

peek
to look at something quickly and secretly
They peeked at the presents under the Christmas tree.

peep
to look at something for a short time, usually when you don't want anyone to see you
Maddy peeped around the corner to see if her brothers were still waiting for her.

• to look at something for a long time

gaze
to look at someone or something for a long time, usually with a good feeling
We gazed up at the stars in the sky.

glare
to stare angrily at someone or something
They glared at each other.

glare

stare
to look directly at someone or something without moving your eyes away
It's rude to stare.

• to look at something or someone carefully

examine
to look at something very carefully, usually to discover something
They examined the fossils closely.

inspect
to look at something carefully, to make sure it is safe or correct
They inspect all the tyres.

peer
to look carefully at something, because you can't see it very well
They peered into the cave.

study
to look at something carefully, to learn or understand something
Study the map closely.

Loud

blaring • booming • deafening

• very loud

blaring
making a loud noise
The song starts with blaring horns and loud drums.

booming
very loud and deep
We could hear Joe's booming voice from outside.

deafening
so loud that you can't hear anything else
The explosion was deafening.

> The opposites of loud are soft and low.

thunderous
extremely loud
When the music stopped, the applause was thunderous.

• unpleasantly loud

ear-splitting
so loud that it hurts your ears
The fire alarm is ear-splitting.

▶ ear-splitting

noisy
loud in an unpleasant way
It's noisy in the swimming pool today.

ar-splitting • noisy • penetrating
piercing • rowdy • thunderous

In other words

Sometimes we use 'loud' to describe things such as clothes that are unpleasantly colourful.

Word partners

Loud and clear
something that is obvious and easy to understand
We understood the message loud and clear.

penetrating
loud, clear and unpleasant
The ship's horn gives a penetrating blast.

piercing
loud and high-pitched
She's got such a piercing voice, it went straight through me.

⚠ piercing

rowdy
people who are noisy and quite badly behaved
A few of the team were rowdy last night.

• to love someone

be close to
to love someone you can talk to easily
I'm very close to my older sister.

be fond of
to like someone very much
They're very fond of each other.

care about
to feel concerned about and like someone
We care about all children, everywhere.

be close to

• to love someone or something very much

adore
to really love someone or something
Molly adores chocolate.

adore

be devoted to
to love and be loyal to someone
My grandparents are devoted to each other.

be devoted to • be fond of • care about
doting • passionate • tender • worship

The opposite of love is hate.

worship
to love or admire someone or something very much
He worships the basketball team!

• feeling or showing love for someone or something

affectionate
showing love
Our baby brother is very affectionate.

doting
showing love by paying attention to someone
They are doting grandparents.

passionate
a very strong feeling of love or devotion
She felt passionately about saving endangered animals.

tender
gentle and loving
She gave the children a tender look as she tucked them into bed.

Word partners

fall in love
to become very fond of someone or something

love at first sight
to fall in love immediately

Make

assemble • build • concoct • create

assemble

to put together the parts of something

We have to assemble the desk from a kit.

build

to make something by putting parts together

They're building a clubhouse for kids only.

concoct

to make something strange to eat or drink

The wizard concocted a magic potion.

▶ concoct

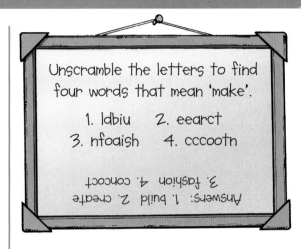

Unscramble the letters to find four words that mean 'make'.

1. ldbiu   2. eearct
3. nfoaish   4. cccootn

Answers: 1. build 2. create 3. fashion 4. concoct

create

to make something that wasn't there before

Our class created a sculpture for the park.

fashion

to make something to do a particular job

The castaway fashioned a sail for the raft.

A B C D E F G H I J K L M

form
to make (or be a part of) something
Water is formed from hydrogen and oxygen.

manufacture
to make something, especially in a factory
They manufacture toys.

mould
to shape a substance, such as clay or wax
Wax is moulded into candles.

In other words

cobble something together
(idiom)
to make something roughly and quickly
We didn't have a real go-cart but we cobbled something together.

produce
to make something
Spring is the time when many plants produce flowers.

generate
to make something by using a process
The power station generates electricity.

The opposite of make is destroy.

Mistake

• a mistake

blunder
a stupid or clumsy mistake
It was a foolish blunder.

error
a serious mistake you don't know
you're making
*They made an error when they charged
us for the meal.*

fault
a mistake, usually that someone
or something is to blame for
*I think the entire system of filing
information is at fault.*

gaffe
an embarrassing mistake
*Putting sugar on your eggs in the
restaurant was a real gaffe.*

oversight
a mistake you make by forgetting
or not noticing something
*Everyone should have been invited –
leaving their names off was an oversight.*

slip

slip
a small mistake that is easy
to correct
It was just a slip of the tongue.

misjudge
to make a mistake by deciding to do the wrong thing
They misjudged the situation.

mix-up
to make a mistake that confuses things
We were supposed to play yesterday but there was a mix-up with the dates.

In other words

put your foot in it (idiom)
to say something stupid or secret that you shouldn't have said
You really put your foot in it when you mentioned the surprise party!

• **to make a mistake**

goof
to make a silly mistake
I goofed the answer.

Money

cash
notes and coins used as money
Do you have any cash with you?

change
money that you get back when you pay for something
Make sure you check your change.

coins
small pieces of metal used as money
Some vending machines only take coins, not notes.

currency
the type of money that is used in a country
The dollar is the currency in Canada, the USA and Australia.

• a lot of money

a fortune
a very large amount of money
What a fantastic idea! We should be able to make a fortune.

In other words

money doesn't grow on trees (idiom)
often used if money is in short supply, or to explain that you should spend money wisely
No, you can't have a new bike — money doesn't grow on trees you know!

A B C D E F G H I J K L **M**

wealth

a large amount of money
The king had great wealth.

• **amounts of money**

figure

an exact amount of money
The figure we decided on is £34.98.

sum

an amount of money
It added up to a good sum.

• **money that someone gives to another person**

allowance

money someone receives regularly, not for working
The allowance from her parents covers basic living expenses.

income

money that people receive, usually from working
Our joint income means we can afford to go on holiday.

pocket money

money that children receive from their parents each week
I work for my dad on Saturdays to earn pocket money.

Did you know?

The word 'money' probably comes from Moneta, a name given to the Roman goddess Juno, whose temple was used to store valuable things.

Move

budge
to move a little way
This is stuck, it won't budge.

relocate
to move something permanently
to another place
*We're moving house – Dad's firm
has relocated to another city.*

shift
to move from one place to another
We shifted the sofa out of the way.

transfer
to move from one place to another
The player transferred to another team.

transport
to take people or goods from one
place to another
The new cars are transported by rail.

**• people or animals moving
their bodies**

squirm
to move your body from side to
side because you are uncomfortable
Stop squirming and sit still.

stir
to move sightly
*She stirred slightly in her sleep but
didn't wake up.*

stir

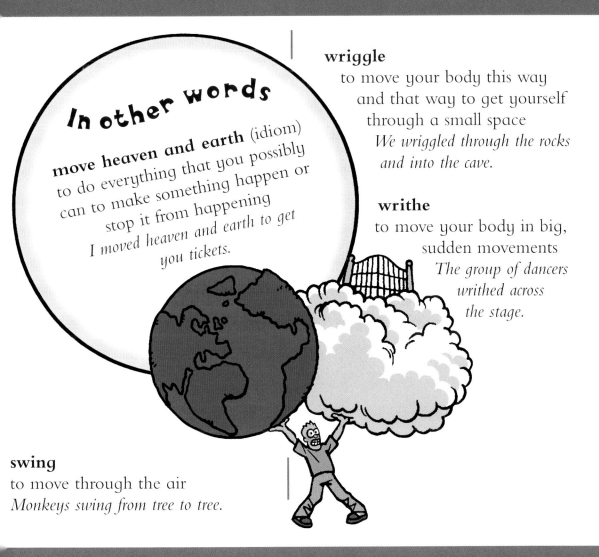

In other words

move heaven and earth (idiom)
to do everything that you possibly can to make something happen or stop it from happening
I moved heaven and earth to get you tickets.

wriggle
to move your body this way and that way to get yourself through a small space
We wriggled through the rocks and into the cave.

writhe
to move your body in big, sudden movements
The group of dancers writhed across the stage.

swing
to move through the air
Monkeys swing from tree to tree.

Name

• people's names

identity
a person's name
The police are keeping his identity a secret.

initial
the first letter of each of your names
Her initials are BJH.

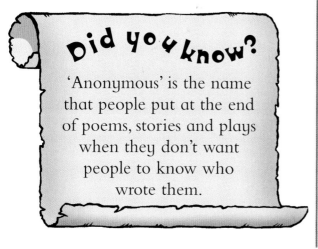

Did you know?

'Anonymous' is the name that people put at the end of poems, stories and plays when they don't want people to know who wrote them.

maiden name
a married woman's surname before she was married
These days, many women keep their maiden names after they get married.

namesake

namesake
a person who has the same name as you, especially a famous person
Our dog's namesake is Beckham.

A B C D E F G H I J K L M

nickname
a name your friends or family call you
Her nickname is Bizzy.

• false names

alias
a different name someone is known by, especially a criminal
He was living here under an alias.

pen name
another name writers use instead of their own names
Mark Twain is the pen name of Samuel Clemens.

pseudonym
a name used by someone instead of their real name
Singers and actors sometimes use pseudonyms.

• names for things

brand name
the name a company gives a product
Playstation® is a brand name.

code name
a secret name for someone or something
The army called the new project Operation Storm Cloud.

pen name

N O P Q R S T U V W X Y Z

Near

close • handy • in the vicinity • local • nearby

close
very near
The swimming pool is close to home.

handy
conveniently near
The shop is just around the corner from our house, which is handy.

in the vicinity
in the area around a place
Police believe the thief is still in the vicinity.

🔺 in the vicinity

local
near a place, in an area
Can you tell me where the local post office is?

nearby
near where you are
Is there a leisure centre nearby?

In other words

on your doorstep (idiom)
very near the place where you live
Sam likes living in a city because everything is on his doorstep.

A B C D E F G H I J K L M

neighbouring

near the place where you live or the place you are talking about
The secondary school is in the neighbouring village.

next

the one that is closest
My best friend lives in the house next door.

The opposite of near is far.

surrounding

near and around a place
There are two supermarkets in the surrounding area.

within walking distance

close enough to walk to easily
We have a cinema within walking distance of our house.

◁ next

N O P Q R S T U V W X Y Z

New

brand new • fresh • innovative • just out

brand new
completely new
We've just bought a brand new car.

just out
very new
Have you heard their latest album, it's just out on CD?

latest
the most recent
I've just bought the latest version of the game.

modern
up to date
The modern houses on the estate make ours seem very old-fashioned in comparison.

brand new

fresh
clean, new and not used
The tennis players asked for fresh balls.

innovative
new, different and better
The skateboard is an innovative design.

The opposite of new is old.

A B C D E F G H I J K L M

In other words

hot off the press (idiom)
the latest news
This is the news from the Olympics – hot off the press.

novel
something that is new, interesting and different
Our teacher said having hot drinks at break was a novel idea.

original
new, not done before
He had original ideas about the building work.

pioneering
done for the first time
Marie Curie carried out pioneering research in the science world.

recent
something that was made or done a short time ago
We are looking for recent articles about the zoo.

newcomer
a person who has recently arrived in a place
The family are newcomers to the town.

N O P Q R S T U V W X Y Z

• things that are old

ancient
extremely old, existing many years ago
Archimedes was a scientist in ancient Greece.

ancient

antique
old and valuable
My grandfather gave me an antique pocket watch.

In other words

as old as the hills (idiom)
very old
That joke is as old as the hills!

second-hand
owned by someone else before you
Charity shops sell second-hand clothes.

used
not new, or owned by someone else before
Used computers for sale are advertised in the local newspaper.

vintage
old and one of the best of its type
Vintage wine is very expensive.

• people who are old

ageing
becoming older
The UK has an ageing population.

elderly
old
*Gran
is quite
elderly but
she still likes
to go cycling
with us.*

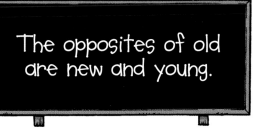

The opposites of old
are new and young.

to be getting on
getting older
Grandad is getting on a bit.

veteran
old and experienced
Dad plays on the veteran team.

• things or places for people
who are old

geriatric
to do with old people
*Geriatrics is the branch of medicine
concerned with elderly people.*

elderly

Open

force
to open something that is stuck or locked by pushing hard on it
The firefighters forced the lift doors open.

pick a lock
to open a lock with something that is not a key
Car locks are extra safe so thieves can't pick the locks.

prise

prise
to force something apart to open it
The trunk was prised open.

Word partners

an open mind
Not decided in advance
He kept an open mind about the holiday.

unbolt
to open a door or gate by sliding a metal bar across
Carefully unbolt the door and lead the pony out.

unfold
to open paper or cloth and spread it out
Unfold the map and try to find out where we are.

A B C D E F G H I J K L M

unlock
to open a lock using a key
Can you unlock the door? My hands are full.

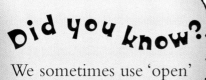

Did you know?
We sometimes use 'open' to describe people who are honest and happy to talk about things.

unscrew
to take the top off a container by turning it
If you can't unscrew something, try using a cloth to hold it.

unwrap
to open a parcel by taking paper or cloth off it
We can't wait to unwrap our presents on Christmas morning.

• **to be open**

ajar
slightly open
If the door is ajar, just go straight in.

wide open
completely open
We left the garage door wide open by mistake.

 ajar

Ordinary

average
typical, like most others of the same type
An average lesson lasts 45 minutes.

banal
ordinary, not interesting or new
Some people think the words in pop songs are banal.

bland
boring, dull or not tasty
Bland foods are not spicy.

commonplace
an everyday happening or sight
Red buses are commonplace in the city.

everyday
not unusual or special
The Internet is a part of everyday life now.

mundane
ordinary and dull
Cleaning the rabbit's cage is a mundane task.

mundane

neutral
plain, without strong colours, flavours or opinions
I've painted the entire house in neutral colours.

normal
like other people or things of the same type
His height and weight are normal for his age.

routine
usual and done frequently
It's just a routine dental check-up.

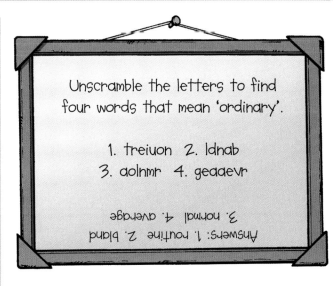

Unscramble the letters to find four words that mean 'ordinary'.

1. treiuon 2. ldnab
3. aolnmr 4. geaaevr

Answers: 1. routine 2. bland
3. normal 4. average

standard
something basic without extra features
The company has a standard document for sending emails.

typical
usual
They really are just a typical family trying to make ends meet.

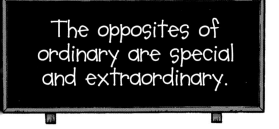

The opposites of ordinary are special and extraordinary.

N O P Q R S T U V W X Y Z

bit
a small part
Would you like to taste a bit of this chocolate bar?

branch
an office or shop that is part of a big organisation
Mum works in the local branch of the bank.

component
part of a machine or system
The hard disk is a component of computers.

cross−section
a part of something that is cut or divided to show how the rest works or looks
This cross-section shows the different layers of skin.

crumb
a small bit of bread or cake
Who ate all the cake? There are only crumbs left!

△ crumb

element
one of the separate parts of something
Different levels are an important element of any good computer game.

fraction
a small part of an amount or number
We've only raised a fraction of the amount we need.

ingredient
part of a food recipe
Mix all the ingredients together.

The opposites of part are whole and all.

In other words

part and parcel (idiom)
a necessary part of something
Homework is part and parcel of being at school.

portion
part of something larger
A portion of the profit goes to charity.

section
a part of something that is separate from something else
Which section of the school is your classroom in?

segment
a part of something such as fruit
Divide the orange into segments before you put it in the fruit salad.

Payment

• **payment for work or service**

bonus
extra money for working hard
Dad got a bonus for getting a new account.

fee
the amount of money paid for something
The school fees are high.

salary
the total payment someone gets each year for doing a job
Mum's salary is higher now that she has a new job.

wages
the money that someone gets each week for doing a job
Wages are paid every Thursday.

• **payment in a restaurant**

tip
money that you give a waiter for service
Are you going to leave a tip?

tip

• **payment as a punishment**

fine
money paid for breaking the law
We had to pay a parking fine.

A B C D E F G H I J K L M

• payment to get something

bribe

payment to a person so that they will do something, usually against the law
The prisoner bribed the guard to let him out of his cell.

deposit

a payment you make when you decide to buy something, to prove that you will buy it
I've paid a £10 deposit on the CD player I want.

instalment

a partial payment that you make to buy something over a period of time
I paid for the holiday in six monthly instalments.

In other words

pay through the nose
(idiom)
pay too much for something
You have to pay through the nose for some trainers.

refund

money that you get back when you return something, usually to a shop
We got a full refund on the television.

Person

family
a group of people who are related
How many kids are there in your family?

family

folk
people
They're friendly folk.

humanity
all the people who have ever lived
Cave paintings are early records of humanity.

humankind
all the people in the world
This is something for all humankind to be proud of.

individual
one person
Every classroom is made up of unique individuals.

human/human being
a man, woman or child
The gorillas are not used to seeing humans.

kin
members of a family
Next of kin means the person you are most closely related to.

A B C D E F G H I J K L M

hero • heroine • human • human being • humanity
humankind • individual • kin • somebody • someone

Unscramble the letters to find
four family members.

1. ousinc   2. ceine
3. uelnc   4. nweehp

Answers: 1. cousin 2. neice
3. uncle 4. nephew

hero/heroine
the main character in a story, or a
person who does something brave
The hero killed the dragon.

somebody/someone
a person — used when you do not
know the person's name or when it
is not important to use their name
Quick, somebody call an ambulance!

• **people in a story**

character
a person who appears in a book,
film, game or story
Who is your favourite character?

In other words

person in the street (idiom)
ordinary people
We say 'the man or woman in the
street' to talk about what most people
think. Sometimes we
say 'Joe Public' to talk
about the average
person.

Poor

broke • deprived • destitute • disadvantaged

broke
not having any money temporarily
I can't come out tonight, I'm broke until Friday.

deprived
not having the things you need for a normal life
Charles Dickens had a deprived childhood.

The opposite of poor is rich.

destitute
so poor that you do not have basic things such as enough food
The refugees are destitute.

disadvantaged
not having the same opportunities as other people
The charity helps disadvantaged families.

impoverished
made poor
The country was impoverished after many years of drought.

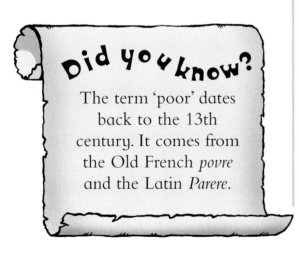

Did you know?

The term 'poor' dates back to the 13th century. It comes from the Old French *povre* and the Latin *Parere*.

A B C D E F G H I J K L M

needy
not having enough money
Anyone who is needy is welcome to come for a free meal.

underprivileged
poor and with fewer opportunities than other people
We collect aluminium cans to raise money for underprivileged families.

penniless

penniless
without any money
The winning lottery ticket was found by a penniless beggar.

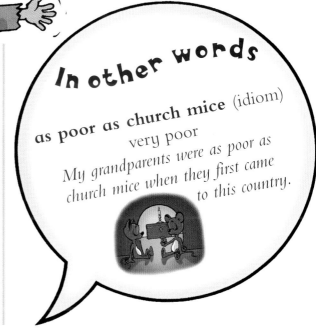

In other words

as poor as church mice (idiom)
very poor
My grandparents were as poor as church mice when they first came to this country.

Pretend

artificial • bluff • fake • false

• to pretend

bluff
to pretend that you will do something or that you know something
Do you really know the answer or are you just bluffing?

impersonate
to pretend you are someone else
He was arrested for impersonating a policeman.

masquerade
to dress up in a disguise
They masqueraded as children.

pose as
to pretend to be someone else
She was posing as the head of the committee.

• not real

artificial
not real or not natural
The coats were made with artificial fur.

fake/false
something that pretends to look similar to something else
Are you wearing false eyelashes?

▼ false

A B C D E F G H I J K L M

In other words

to cry crocodile tears
(idiom)
to pretend to be upset
Your crocodile tears don't fool me.

make-believe
not real
The film is just make-believe.

• **people who pretend**

impostor
a person who pretends to be someone else
The king was really an impostor.

Did you know?

In England in 1491, Perkin Warbeck pretended to be one of the Princes in the Tower, who had supposedly been murdered by their uncle, Richard III.

insincere
not really meaning what you say
His apology sounded very insincere

Problem

catch
a hidden problem
There is a catch for arriving so late: you have to work through your lunch hour today.

complication
a problem that makes a situation more difficult
I will be on time unless there are complications.

difficulty
a problem that is not easy to deal with
I'm having difficulty choosing which car to buy.

dilemma
a very difficult choice
We have a major dilemma – we can go out, but we have to take my little brother with us.

In other words

stumbling block (idiom)
a problem that is likely to stop someone from doing what they want to do
Time may be the stumbling block.

hassle

an annoying problem
We had a bit of hassle getting the dog into the car.

hassle

hiccup

a small problem that is quickly solved
There was a minor hiccup but nothing serious to worry about.

hindrance

something that stops you from doing something easily
I was trying to wash our car but the rain was a real hindrance.

hurdle

a problem that you have to solve so that you can do what you are trying to do
The team has had to overcome several hurdles: injuries, player moves and lack of funds.

snag

a difficulty
The snag is, tickets are very expensive.

hindrance

Promise

assure • deliver • give your word

• to make a promise

assure
to say that something is true or that something will happen to make someone feel better
The vet assured us nothing was wrong.

give your word (of honour)
to make a very serious promise
He gave his word that he would return.

guarantee
to say that something is true or that something will happen because you are very sure about it
I guarantee there won't be any problems.

pledge
to say that you will do something or give something
We pledged £5 for the sponsored walk.

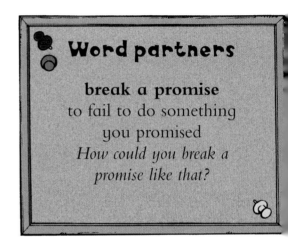

Word partners

break a promise
to fail to do something you promised
How could you break a promise like that?

swear
to make a promise that something is true, sometimes officially
If I tell you a secret, do you swear not to tell anyone?

undertake
an official or legal promise
The government has undertaken to reduce poverty.

vow
to make a serious promise or decision
We vowed to be friends forever.

• to fulfil a promise

deliver
to do what you promised
Will they be able to deliver as promised?

go through with
to keep a promise, especially if you no longer want to or think you can
I don't think we can win the match but we will go through with it anyway.

stand by/stick to
to keep a promise even though the situation has changed
The directors said they would stand by their promise.

In other words

promise the earth (idiom)
to promise something that is impossible
My brother promised us the earth if we would just be quiet.

Proud

arrogant
overly proud of yourself, acting as though you are more important than other people
He is arrogant and rude.

bigheaded
feeling that you are very clever, especially because you have been successful at something
Since Jemma was made head girl, she's acting really bigheaded.

bigheaded

boastful
talking proudly about things you have or have done
He can't open his mouth without being boastful.

conceited
overly proud of your abilities, looks or the things you have done
It's difficult to be friends with a conceited person.

haughty
proud and unfriendly
I thought she was haughty but she's really just shy.

pompous
trying to impress people with how important you are
It was a pompous speech.

> The opposite of proud is ashamed.

A B C D E F G H I J K L M

In other words

too big for your boots (idiom)
believing that you are more important than you really are
You're getting too big for your boots. You can't tell me what to do!

superior
thinking that you are better than other people
It's difficult to learn from people who think they are superior.

vain
thinking that you are very good-looking
Stop looking in the mirror, you vain thing!

smug
too pleased with yourself
He won't be so smug when he finds out that he came second this time.

snobbish
thinking that you are better than someone else because you are in a higher social position
Snobbish people aren't wanted here.

vain

Put

apply
to put a liquid such as paint on something
Apply a thin layer and allow to dry completely.

deposit
to put something somewhere
He deposited the book on the table with a thump.

lay
to put something down flat on a surface
Lay the coats on the bed, please.

⬛ deposit

placc
to put something somewhere carefully
Place the stencil on the paper.

position
to carefully move something into a certain position
Position the prism at an angle.

• to put something against something else

lean
to put something against a wall or other vertical surface
Lean the ladder against the wall.

prop
to lean something against something else for support
I'll prop my bike against the wall.

A B C D E F G H I J K L M

pile • place • position • prop • stack • stand

stand
to lean something against a wall
so that it is nearly vertical
*Stand the picture in the corner for
a minute.*

• to put things on top of one
another

Can you unscramble these
four words that mean 'put'?

1. lapce   2. tacks
3. yal   4. leip

Answers: 1. place 2. stack
3. lay 4. pile

heap
to throw or drop things on top of
each other in an untidy way
He just heaps his clothes on the floor.

pile
to put things on top of each other
Pile the books on the table.

stack
to put things carefully on top
of one another
The CDs are stacked in the cupboard.

heap

N O P Q R S T U V W X Y Z

Quiet

hushed
quiet on purpose
The conversation in the waiting room was hushed.

inaudible
so quiet that you cannot hear it
He spoke in an almost inaudible whisper.

low
quiet and deep
There was a low hum coming from the machine.

muffled
quiet and unclear or blurred
Their speech is muffled by the helmets they are wearing.

The opposites of quiet are noisy and loud.

muted
quieter than usual
We could hear muted voices in the corridor.

silent
with no sound
Please be absolutely silent while we are recording.

◁ muffled

A B C D E F G H I J K L M

soft
quiet and pleasant
There is soft music playing in the background.

still
calm and quiet
The night was still and the sky was full of stars.

Word partners

peace and quiet
usually used when someone wants to escape a noisy or stressful situation
I'm going out to get some peace and quiet.

In other words
as quiet as a mouse (idiom)
very quiet
I didn't hear you come in, you were as quiet as a mouse.

subdued
quieter than usual because you are sad or worried
You seem a bit subdued today – are you okay?

taciturn
saying very little
He plays the part of a stern, taciturn man.

Real

• not false

authentic
real or true
This is an authentic antique map.

bona fide
real and honest
Make sure it's a bona fide website before you buy anything online.

genuine
not a fake
Genuine leather lasts a long time.

true
not a lie
It's true, the dog really did eat my homework!

true

> The opposites of real are false and imaginary.

• real feelings

heartfelt
strong and truly meant
Please accept our heartfelt thanks.

sincere
real and truly felt
I trust her and think she is being completely sincere.

• **existing, not imaginary**

actual
real
Her nickname is Posh but her actual name is Victoria.

concrete
based on facts
Do the police have any concrete evidence?

concrete

solid
based on real facts
There is solid evidence that smoking is bad for you.

In other words

The Real McCoy (idiom)
the real thing, not a copy
This comes from an American boxer, Kid McCoy, who was called The Real McCoy.

Remember

• **to remember**

recall
to remember
something
on purpose
*As I recall, we
said we'd meet at
the sports centre.*

relive
to remember something
very clearly
*I relived missing that goal so
many times!*

◀ relive

reminisce
to think or talk about nice things
from the past
*My parents like to reminisce about
living in Africa.*

recollect
to be able to remember something
*We went to Greece when I was a small
child but I don't recollect anything
about it.*

> The opposite of
> remember is forget.

• **to cause someone to
remember**

prompt
to help someone remember
something, especially an actor
in a play
I'll prompt you if you forget the lines.

A B C D E F G H I J K L M

recall • recollect • relive • remind
reminisce • unforgettable

remind
to make someone remember
something they need to
know or do
*Remind me to leave
a note for the
milkman.*

• **easy to
remember**

▶ haunting

haunting
easy to remember in a mysterious
way
*A beautiful, haunting melody
keeps going through my head.*

memorable
easy to remember because it is
very special
*Meeting the royal family was a
memorable moment.*

unforgettable
easy to remember because it
affected you a lot
*My first day at the new school
was unforgettable.*

In other words

something rings a bell (idiom)
something makes you partly
remember something
James? The name rings a bell.

rack your brains (idiom)
try to remember something
*Where are we going on
holiday? I've been racking
my brains trying to
remember.*

N O P Q R S T U V W X Y Z

affluent
having a lot of money to buy things with
This is an affluent neighbourhood.

comfortable
having enough money
My grandparents have a comfortable life.

prosperous
successful and having a lot of money
The town has become prosperous since the factory was built.

▶ flush

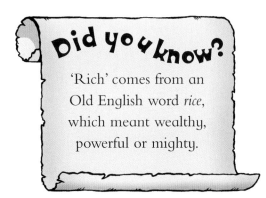

Did you know?

'Rich' comes from an Old English word *rice*, which meant wealthy, powerful or mighty.

flush
having more money than you usually have
I'll treat you – I'm flush right now.

A B C D E F G H I J K L M

comfortable • flush • prosperous • the haves
wealthy • well-heeled • well-off

In other words

to be rolling in it (idiom)
to be very rich
Most pop stars are absolutely rolling in it!

wealthy
rich
They are a wealthy family and they're very generous.

well-heeled
having a lot of money and nice clothes
They look well-heeled.

well-off
having more money than most people
They're quite a well-off couple.

• **people who are rich**

a man/woman of means
a person who is rich and has property
The racehorse owner is a man of means.

the haves
people who have money
Unfortunately, there are still the haves and have-nots.

The opposite of rich is poor.

N O P Q **R** S T U V W X Y Z

Right

accepted
approved or agreed that something
is right
*It is an accepted fact that the world is
not flat.*

> The opposite of
> right is wrong.

In other words

**to be in the right place at the
right time** (idiom)
to be in a place or a position where
something good is offered
*She's so lucky – always in the right
place at the right time.*

accurate
completely correct and true
*You have to type in web
addresses accurately.*

appropriate
right for a certain situation
*It's not appropriate to wear pyjamas
to school.*

apt
exactly right or suitable for
a situation
*Several pupils made apt remarks during
the discussion.*

A B C D E F G H I J K L M

correct
with no mistakes
Use the key to check that your answers are correct.

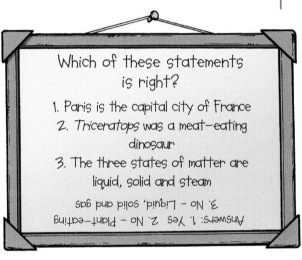

Which of these statements is right?

1. Paris is the capital city of France
2. *Triceratops* was a meat-eating dinosaur
3. The three states of matter are liquid, solid and steam

Answers: 1. Yes 2. No – Plant-eating 3. No – Liquid, solid and gas

fitting
suitable or right for a particular situation
The poem was fitting for the ceremony.

just
fair, morally right
It was a just punishment for the crime.

proper
right or correct
Put the books in the proper order.

suitable
right for a particular situation or time
Trainers aren't suitable shoes to wear to a wedding.

▶ suitable

Run

bolt
to run or move quickly because you are frightened
The horse bolted when the bell rang.

▼ bolt

dash
to run fast for a short distance
It was raining so we dashed to the car.

flee
to run away from danger
The children were fleeing from the monsters.

gallop
to run quickly with big steps
He galloped around the house.

jog
to run quite slowly for quite a long way
Mum jogs three times a week.

lope
to run with long, relaxed strides
The highjumper loped up to the bar and sprang over it with ease.

◀ flee

A B C D E F G H I J K L M

race

to run fast, especially against someone in a competition
We raced around the school field as fast as we could.

rush

move quickly to get somewhere or do something in a hurry
Mum was rushing around the house looking for her keys.

sprint

to run as fast as you can
The team of athletes sprinted around the track.

tear

to run fast without watching where you're going
He tore around the corner of the building and straight into the teacher.

race

Word partners

run for cover

to move quickly to find shelter
As the rain began, we ran for cover.

Sad

down/low
sad and without energy
You might feel a little bit down after you've had flu.

fed-up
unhappy and annoyed or bored
I'm fed-up waiting for you.

glum

glum
sad-looking
Why the glum face?

homesick
sad because you are away from home and miss the people there
You'll be homesick for the first few days.

unhappy
sad because of something that happens
What's wrong? You look unhappy.

• very sad

dejected
sad and disappointed
We were dejected when we lost.

The opposite of sad is happy.

A B C D E F G H I J K L M

despondent • down • fed-up • glum
homesick • low • miserable • unhappy

depressed
feeling sad, usually for a long time
I was quite depressed when we first moved here but now I really like it.

desolate
extremely sad and lonely
The area has a flat, desolate landscape.

despondent
very sad and disappointed or not hopeful about the future
The team is despondent – they haven't won a match all year.

miserable
extremely sad
When you feel miserable you should just get up and do something.

In other words

sadder but wiser (idiom)
to have learned something from a bad or difficult experience
We came back from the match sadder but wiser.

N O P Q R S T U V W X Y Z

consistent
steady, staying the same
Jess has made consistent improvement this term.

verbatim
in exactly the same words as the original
It is a verbatim account of the trial.

word for word
using exactly the same words
She repeated his speech, word for word.

• something that is the same as something else

carbon copy
exactly like another thing
The puppies are carbon copies of their mother.

carbon copy

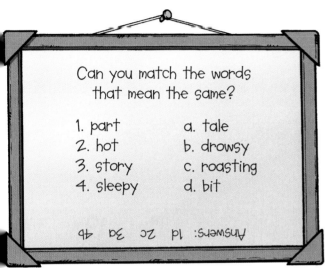

Can you match the words
that mean the same?

1. part   a. tale
2. hot   b. drowsy
3. story   c. roasting
4. sleepy   d. bit

Answers: 1d 2c 3a 4b

equivalent
something that has the same
amount or size as something else
*Do you know what the equivalent
of £10 is in euros?*

identical
exactly the same
That jacket is identical to mine.

synonym
a word that means the same
as another word
*Sidewalk is the American synonym
of pavement.*

counterpart
someone who has the same position
as someone else
The minister met his UK counterpart.

duplicate
something that is an exact copy of
something else
Please keep a duplicate of the letter.

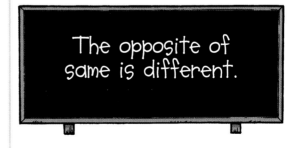

The opposite of
same is different.

N O P Q R S T U V W X Y Z

Say

blurt out
to say something without thinking
He blurted out the answer.

hint
to say something indirectly
Mr Hunt hinted that there would be a test.

▶ blurt out

comment
to give an opinion
The captain commented on each player's performance.

exclaim
to say something loudly or suddenly
"This ride is fantastic!" she exclaimed.

mention
to say a little bit about a fact
The head mentioned that there would be new pupils this term.

A B C D E F G H I J K L M

In other words

it goes without saying
(idiom)
so obvious that something does not actually have to be said
It goes without saying that he'll do a good job.

remark
to say what you think about something
The reporter remarked on how good our school's website is.

tell
to say something to someone
Please don't tell anyone.

whisper
to say something very softly
You play the game by whispering the sentence to the person next to you.

mumble
to say something unclearly
Don't mumble when you're on stage, speak clearly.

whisper

mutter
to say something quietly, especially if you are complaining
One of the players muttered something about the referee.

behind someone's back
done without telling someone
Friends don't do things behind your back.

cagey
not willing to tell other people your plans
Dad's being a bit cagey about where we're going on holiday – he wants it to be a surprise.

clandestine
something that is secret and sometimes illegal
The group holds clandestine meetings.

In other words

between you, me and the gatepost (idiom)
what you say when you tell someone something you don't want anyone else to know
Now, this is just between you, me and the gatepost.

clandestine • concealed • confidential • covert
furtive • hidden • hush-hush • in private

Word partners

keep a secret
to not tell anyone a secret
someone has told you
Can you keep a secret?

concealed
not showing
The microphone is concealed in a lamp.

confidential
private
The report is highly confidential.

covert
done in a secret way
We are involved in covert operations.

furtive
in a secret way
It was a quick, furtive pass.

hidden
not shown or visible
There's a message hidden in the book.

hush-hush
very secret
The plans are all very hush-hush.

in private
done where other people cannot
see or hear
They will discuss it in private.

The opposite of
secret is public.

N O P Q R S T U V W X Y Z

Sleep

catnap
a very short sleep, usually not very deep
Why don't you have a quick catnap before we leave for the airport?

doze
to sleep lightly
I was just dozing in front of the TV.

drift off
to go to sleep slowly
Be quiet, we're hoping the baby will drift off.

▶ drift off

The opposite of asleep is awake.

drop off
to go to sleep easily
I dropped off as soon as my head hit the pillow.

hibernate (for animals)
to go to sleep during the winter
Bears sometimes hibernate in caves.

kip
a short sleep
Why don't you have a kip in the car?

A B C D E F G H I J K L M

nap

a short sleep, usually in the afternoon

Grandma has a nap after lunch.

slumber

sleep

The princess ate the apple and fell into a deep slumber.

Word partners

light sleeper

someone whose sleep is easily disturbed

Mum's a light sleeper.

In other words

to sleep like a log

(idiom)

to sleep very well

Did you get some sleep?

Yeah, I slept like a log!

snooze

a short, light sleep

Dad had a snooze while we went out for a walk.

Small

dainty
small and delicate
The doll has dainty hands.

The opposite of
small is large.

little
not big
They live in a sweet little cottage.

meagre
not enough, too little
The farmers try to survive on their meagre harvest.

miniature
much smaller than normal
There is a miniature town in Denmark.

minuscule
very small
A baby panda is minuscule compared to its mother.

minute
very small and difficult to see
A cat's whiskers are covered in minute sensors.

puny

puny
small and weak
Pat Rafter was puny when he was a boy.

become smaller

In other words

small world
something you say when you meet someone who knows a person or a place you know, and you are surprised
I don't believe you've met Sally too – what a small world!

shrink
to get smaller, often because of the effects of water or heat
My T-shirt shrank in the wash – it's too small now.

shrink

tiny
very small
Coral reefs are made up of thousands of tiny animals.

shrivel
to get smaller and drier
Tomatoes shrivel up in very hot sun.

Smile

- to smile because you are happy

beam
to smile a big smile for a long time, usually because you are proud of something or someone
The parents beamed as their children went up to receive their prizes.

face lights up
to look happy suddenly
Their faces lit up as soon as they saw the lights on the tree.

> **Did you know?**
>
> In Old English, 'smirk' was the word for 'smile', but not in the unpleasant way that we understand it now.

grin
to suddenly break into a wide, happy smile
They grinned and waved when they saw us.

to break into a smile
to suddenly start smiling
She broke into a smile when she heard the good news.

> The opposite of smile is frown.

A B C D E F G H I J K L M

• to smile in an unpleasant way

simper
to smile in a foolish, annoying way
The student simpered at the teacher.

smirk
to smile in a nasty way because you are pleased about someone else's bad luck
What are you smirking about?

sneer
to smile in an unpleasant way that shows that you don't respect someone or something
The giant sneered at the children as he passed by.

In other words

to grin like a Cheshire cat (idiom)
to smile very widely because you're pleased about something
This comes from a character in Lewis Carroll's book *Alice's Adventures in Wonderland*. Alice goes to a land where nothing is normal and she meets many strange characters. The Cheshire cat is one of these. He fades away as Alice is talking to him. The only thing left is his grin, floating in the air.

Start

activate • begin • commence • embark on

activate
to start something happening or working
The machine is activated by pressing this button.

The opposites of start are finish and end.

In other words

to give someone a head start (idiom)
to give someone an advantage
The hare was so confident of winning the race, he gave the tortoise a head start.

begin
to start doing something
You should begin the letter with 'Dear Sir'.

commence
to start or begin
The ceremony will now commence.

embark on
to start a big, important job or a journey
Our school is embarking on a big recycling project.

A B C D E F G H I J K L M

establish • found • initiate • launch
open • set in motion • set up

initiate
to start something such as a discussion about something
A neighbouring country initiated the peace talks.

launch

launch
to start something publicly
The ship was launched by the mayoress.

open
to begin to be shown, such as a film
We want to see the film when it opens.

set in motion
to start something like a process that will take a long time
The plan has been set in motion.

• **to start something in an organization**

establish
to start something permanent
Oxford University was established more than 800 years ago.

found
to start something like a company or city
The company was founded in 1995.

set up
to make all the plans to start something
We've set up everything.

N O P Q R S T U V W X Y Z

Steal

burglar • burgle • kleptomaniac • loot • mug

• to steal

burgle
to steal things from
a place such as a
house or office
*Our house was burgled
last night.*

▶ burgle

poach
to catch animals without
permission
Poaching is a problem in Africa.

rob
to steal something from
a person or place
An armed gang robbed the bank.

shoplift
to steal things from a shop
A boy was caught shoplifting.

loot
to steal things from shops when the
police are busy because something
else is happening
Shops were looted in the riots.

mug
to attack and steal from someone
in the street
*The man was mugged as he walked
home from work.*

Did you know?

The word 'steal'
probably comes from
the Old English *stelan*.

A B C D E F G H I J K L M

In other words

tea leaf
cockney rhyming slang
for 'thief'.

daylight robbery (idiom)
very expensive
*These prices are
daylight robbery.*

• **people who steal**

burglar

a person who steals things
from a building
The burglar got in through a window.

kleptomaniac

a person who is unable to stop
stealing
Kleptomaniacs need professional help.

mugger

a person who steals money from
people by attacking them in the
street
*The mugger was sent to jail for several
months.*

robber

a person who steals things from
a public place
The robbers wore masks.

shoplifter

a person who steals when they
are in shops
*The CCTVs are there to stop
shoplifters.*

thief

a general word for a person who
steals things
Car thieves can steal a car very quickly.

abandon
to stop doing something before it is finished because it is difficult
The team abandoned the search.

> The opposites of stop are start and begin.

cease
to stop happening
Fighting has ceased.

drop
to stop doing something because it does not seem like a good thing to do
We've decided to drop plans for a concert until after the holidays.

end
to finish or stop
How does the story end?

finish
to stop doing something because it is complete
When you finish the test you may leave.

In other words

to stop someone in their tracks (idiom)
to surprise someone suddenly so they stop what they are doing
A loud noise stopped us in our tracks.

halt

halt
to stop moving
The procession halted.

pause
to stop temporarily
Pause, take a breath and then sing the next part.

quit
to stop doing something
Quit running, walk!

retire
to stop working
Grandma retired when she was 60.

stall
to stop, usually an engine in a car or plane, because there is not enough power
Our car sometimes stalls on hills.

Story

anecdote
a short, usually funny, story
He told an anecdote about his first day at school.

epic
a very long story about past times told in a poem, book or film
Beowulf *is an epic poem that was written more than 1000 years ago.*

fable
a story with a moral message, usually with animal characters
Aesop's Fables *were not written down at first.*

legend
a very old magical story
The legend of William Tell is about a man who had to shoot an apple off his son's head.

In other words

to cut a long story short
(idiom)
to tell the main facts of a story leaving out most of the details
Anyway, to cut a long story short, we decided to come home early.

A B C D E F G H I J K L M

Word partners

a tall story
a story that is hard to believe because it is very exciting or unlikely
He tells such tall stories, it is difficult to believe a single word.

myth
an ancient story
There are famous myths from ancient Greece, Rome and Scandinavia.

novel
a book that is about imaginary people and things
Would you like to borrow it — it's an amazing novel?

saga
a story about a long period of time
A saga is often written about one family.

tale
an exciting story
My uncle tells tales about his adventures in Africa.

yarn
a long story about exciting things that are hard to believe
'Spinning yarns' means telling people stories that aren't true.

novel

Stupid

absurd • daft • dim • foolish

• words for describing ideas or other things that are not sensible

absurd
completely stupid
The plan is absolutely absurd – it'll never work.

daft
childishly stupid but sometimes funny
Michael is very bright but sometimes he has daft ideas.

▶ daft

foolish
stupid in a way that could cause problems in the future
I think it would be foolish to plant the seeds this early.

idiotic
very stupid, sometimes risky
He's always taking idiotic chances – he's a real daredevil.

ridiculous
unbelievably stupid
Don't be ridiculous – we can't be in two places at the same time.

A B C D E F G H I J K L M

In other words

to play the fool (idiom)
to act in a silly way to make people laugh
Sam is always playing the fool.

unwise
stupid in a way that could cause problems
It is unwise to swim right after eating a big meal.

• **not intelligent**

dim
slow to understand or learn
Now I get it, sorry to be so dim!

thick
not intelligent at all
He's not thick, just a little confused.

silly
childishly stupid, sometimes in a funny way
We played a few silly games but they were fun.

> The opposites of stupid are sensible and intelligent.

Surprised

- surprised

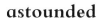

amazed

astounded
very surprised
We were astounded by the news.

shocked
very surprised by something bad
We were shocked by their behaviour.

amazed
so surprised you can't quite
believe what's happened
*We were amazed by some
of his card tricks.*

astonished
very surprised that
something has happened
I'm astonished he won.

In other words

**you could have knocked me
down with a feather!** (idiom)
something you say when you are
really surprised
*You could have
knocked me down
with a feather when
the lights came on and
everybody shouted
"Surprise"!*

incredible • marvellous • shocked • speechless
staggering • stunning • taken aback

speechless

to be so surprised that you can't talk

When they told us the price we were speechless.

taken aback

so surprised that you don't know what to say

I was really taken aback by their comments.

• surprising

incredible

unbelievably surprising

He is an incredible runner.

marvellous

wonderful and surprising

The wildlife photography in this book is marvellous.

speechless

staggering

extremely surprising in a good or bad way

They spent a staggering amount of money.

stunning

very surprising

The special effects are stunning.

N O P Q R S T U V W X Y Z

Take

carry

to take something from one place to another
The helicopter carried fresh supplies of food and water to the camp.

convey

to take something such as liquid, electricity or gas from one place to another
The blood is conveyed from the heart through the body's arteries.

deliver

to take letters, parcels, newspapers and other things to a place
We had to deliver all of the Christmas cards on foot.

In other words

you can take a horse to water but you can't make him drink
(saying)
this means you can give someone the chance to do something but you can't make them take it.

fetch
to go and get something and take it back to where you started
Could you fetch the children from school on your way back?

transport
to take lots of people or things from one place to another
Oil is transported in tankers.

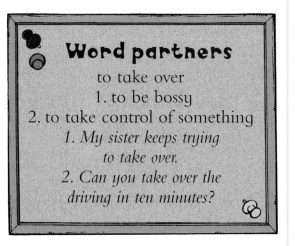

Word partners
to take over
1. to be bossy
2. to take control of something
   1. *My sister keeps trying to take over.*
   2. *Can you take over the driving in ten minutes?*

The opposite of take is give.

• to take someone somewhere

guide
to take someone to a place you know well
We were guided around the exhibition.

lead
to take someone somewhere by going in front of them
They led us out of the cave.

shepherd
to take a group of people somewhere
I was shepherded inside the house.

Talk

blab • chat • converse • gossip

blab
to talk about something that you are not supposed to mention
Who blabbed?

chat
to talk in a friendly way
We were just chatting about what we did in the summer holidays.

converse
to talk to someone
Parents' day is a time when teachers and parents meet and converse.

gossip

Did you know?
'Talk' dates back to the 12th century. It is related to the Middle English word 'tale', which means 'story'.

gossip
to talk about other people's lives
I could tell they were gossiping about something when we walked in.

natter
to talk about things for fun
We sat and nattered about our favourite bands all day long.

A B C D E F G H I J K L M

rabbit
to keep talking about something,
usually boring
What are you rabbiting about now?

waffle
to talk about something without
saying anything useful
He waffled on about badges.

Word partners

small talk
to make polite conversation
about nothing in particular
*The taxi driver made small talk as
he drove us to the station.*

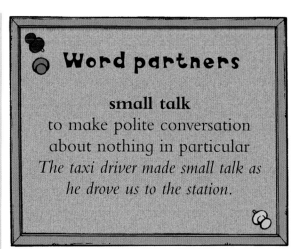

In other words

**can talk the hind
legs off a donkey**
(idiom)
able to talk a lot
*My Aunt Jo can talk
the hind legs
off a donkey.*

witter
to talk for a long
time without saying
much
*Jamie wittered on for
hours.*

Think

brood
to keep thinking about something that upsets you
Don't just sit there brooding – do something about it.

◀ brood

consider
to think about something that you might do
We're considering going to France.

contemplate
to think seriously or deeply about something
They contemplated major changes.

meditate
to think deeply about something for a long time
Meditating each day is really relaxing.

ponder
to think about a difficult question or a problem
He looked at the iron gate and pondered his escape.

reckon
to think that something is right or true
I reckon they'll get here in time.

reflect
to think carefully about something
We need time to reflect on what has happened.

▶ meditate

A B C D E F G H I J K L M

regard
to have an opinion of someone or something
They don't think of it as work – they regard it as good fun.

wonder
to try to guess what is happening or what will happen
I wonder where they've got to?

Did you know?
'Use your loaf' is cockney rhyming slang. It comes from 'loaf of bread', which rhymes with 'head'.

In other words
great minds think alike
(saying)
to have the same thought or idea as someone else

suspect
to think that something is probably true
I suspect there will be a question about gravity in the test.

Throw

bowl
to throw a ball at a batman in cricket
Who's bowling for their team?

chuck
to throw something carelessly
Just chuck that stuff on the floor.

chuck

fling
to throw or move something forcefully
She flung her scarf around her neck.

In other words

to throw in the towel (idiom)
to stop doing something because you don't think you can succeed
The boxer grew tired of fighting and threw in the towel.

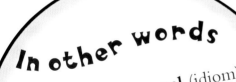

heave
to throw something heavy
They heaved the sacks onto the back of the truck.

hurl
to throw something forcefully and violently
He hurled the spear at the target.

A B C D E F G H I J K L M

lob
to throw something high into the air
We lobbed the ball over the fence.

pass
to throw the ball to another player on the same team
Quick, pass it over here!

pass

pelt

pelt
to throw things at someone or something
The clowns pelted each other with tomatoes.

sling
to throw something carelessly
Don't just sling the book on the table.

toss
to throw something with a quick, small movement
Toss me that cushion, will you?

N O P Q R S T U V W X Y Z

Tired

beat • drained • drowsy • exhausted

beat
so tired that you want to stop what you're doing
Sorry, I've got to rest, I'm beat.

drained
tired, without any energy left
I felt drained after karate class.

drowsy
tired and sleepy
The heat made us drowsy so we went up to bed.

 drained

In other words

to be sick and tired of something (idiom)
to feel angry or bored because something has been happening for a long time
I'm sick and tired of all this ironing.

A B C D E F G H I J K L M

exhausted
very tired
after doing
something that
used up your
energy
*You walked all the
way? You must be
exhausted.*

flagging
starting to lose
energy
*During the
tie-break, you could
see she was flagging.*

flagging

shattered
very tired
*I'm absolutely shattered. Is it okay
if we stay at home tonight?*

sleepy
ready to go to sleep
*Go on up to bed,
you look sleepy.*

sleepy

tired/worn out
very tired after a lot
of physical effort
*That's it. We've got to stop running –
I'm tired out.*

weary
to feel tired after doing something
for a long period of time
*We'd been walking all day and were
very weary.*

N O P Q R S T U V W X Y Z

Travel

• to travel

commute

commute
to travel to and from work
Dad commutes to the city every day.

explore
to travel to find out more about
a place
*We'll have time to really explore
the island.*

wander
to travel round without a plan
*Dad hired a car and we just wandered
along the coast for a week.*

• types of travel

crossing
a trip in a boat or a ship across
water from one side to the other
*It was a rough crossing because
of the storm.*

excursion
a short trip to visit a place
We have an excursion every term.

journey
travel from one place to another,
usually far away
The journey was long but interesting.

outing
a short trip or visit to a place,
usually nearby
*There is a class outing on Friday to
the castle.*

journey • outing • tour • trip • voyage • wander

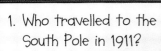

1. Who travelled to the South Pole in 1911?
2. Which space mission travelled to the Moon in 1969?
3. Which aircraft travelled faster than the speed of sound?

Answers: 1. Roald Amundsen 2. Apollo 11 3. Concorde

voyage
a long journey in a ship or spacecraft
We set out on our voyage across the ocean.

tour
a visit to and around a place
We went on a tour of the city.

trip
travel to a place, usually for a short time
Mum is on a business trip.

 voyage

N O P Q R S T U V W X Y Z

Understand

absorb
to learn and understand
new information
*There was a lot of information to absorb
on the first day.*

appreciate
to understand someone's feelings
or their situation
*Teachers appreciate that a child's first
day at school can be confusing.*

comprehend
to understand something difficult
or complicated
*They were
too young to
comprehend what
was happening.*

⏵ digest

Did you know?
We can understand Egyptian
hieroglyphs because of the
Rosetta Stone, found in 1799.
It is an ancient stone with the
same message carved in three
different writing systems.

digest
to think carefully about and
understand new information
They'll need time to digest the report.

follow
to understand something that has
more than one point
Do you follow so far?

A B C D E F G H I J K L M

get

to understand a story, joke or the reason for something
Sorry, but I didn't get that joke.

> The opposite of understand is misunderstand.

grasp

to clearly understand something difficult
They didn't grasp the full importance of the new law.

make sense of

to understand something because you have thought about it
I'm just beginning to make sense of how this computer game works.

realise

to understand something that you didn't before
I didn't realise we were supposed to complete all four questions.

see

to understand what something means or the reason for it
So you see, we need to keep a clear record of each student's project.

Can you understand this text message?

CU L8R R U OK?

Answer: See you later. Are you ok?

Value

• value

advantage
something that is valuable and
will help you succeed
We have a great advantage.

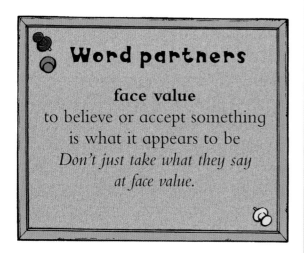

Word partners

face value
to believe or accept something
is what it appears to be
*Don't just take what they say
at face value.*

benefit
something that helps you
We have the benefit of good facilities.

esteem
respect and admiration
Dad's boss holds him in high esteem.

esteem

merit
valuable qualities of something
or someone
The idea has great merit.

worth
the value of something
The thieves took £1000 worth of CDs.

• to value

cherish
to value or love something a lot
Mum cherishes the photos of when we were little.

prize
to feel that something is important or valuable
Grandad prizes his roses.

rate
to give a value to something
I rated the jewellery extremely highly.

treasure
to feel that something is very valuable and gives you a lot of pleasure
We treasure our memories.

• valuable

precious
extremely valuable, usually because it is something that is expensive or rare
Diamonds, emeralds and rubies are all kinds of precious stones.

priceless
so valuable that no price can be put on it
There are lots of priceless Roman artefacts in the museum.

cherish

Very

absolutely • completely • decidedly • highly

absolutely/completely

in every way

I completely forgot to send her a birthday card last year.

decidedly

very much, in an obvious way

The entire team are playing decidedly better this season.

The opposites of very are hardly and slightly.

highly

very

The computer programmers are highly skilled people.

noticeably

very, in a way that is easy for people to see

The sports centre is noticeably busier in the school holidays.

particularly

especially

The judges were particularly impressed with her gymnastic routine.

Did you know?

We don't use 'very' with words that already have a strong meaning. For example, we don't say "I was very astounded." Instead we say something such as, "I was completely astounded."

A B C D E F G H I J K L M

quite
very much
They are twins but their personalities are quite different.

really

really
very
It's really hot in here – can I open the window?

remarkably
very much so, in a surprising way
The results were remarkably good this year.

terribly
very, usually used only in spoken English
I'm terribly sorry I was late – I overslept.

truly
very
I'm truly sorry about the broken window.

truly

N O P Q R S T U V W X Y Z

Wait

await • delay • hesitate

await
to wait for something
The court is awaiting the jury's decision.

hold on
used to tell someone to wait for a short time
Hold on a minute, I'll just check for you.

queue
to stand in a line waiting for something
We had to queue for two hours.

• to wait or make someone wait before doing something

delay
to cause something to be late
We were delayed by traffic.

delay

In other words

he who hesitates is lost
(saying)
If you don't do something when you get the chance, you might not get the chance again.

linger
to wait for extra time before leaving a place
Fans lingered, hoping to get an autograph.

pause
to wait for a while before continuing to do something
The lion paused and looked around.

hesitate
to wait a little while before doing something, usually because you are not sure
Lily hesitated before choosing which library book she wanted.

e	q	r	t	i	r
t	u	o	q	o	e
a	o	d	u	s	g
t	o	e	e	s	n
i	s	l	u	e	i
s	c	a	e	t	l
e	t	y	i	y	u
h	o	p	q	u	e

Find four words that mean 'wait'. They could be backwards!

Answers: hesitate delay linger queue

Walk

creep

to walk quietly, slowly and secretly
We crept up and jumped in front of them.

hike

to walk a long way, usually in the country
We hiked up the hill and found a good place for our picnic.

limp

to walk dragging one foot because it hurts
David limped slowly off the football pitch.

march

to walk together using strong, regular steps
The group of soldiers marched proudly past the flag.

creep

stride

to walk confidently with big steps
He strode into the room.

stroll

to walk slowly and comfortably
We strolled through the park.

A B C D E F G H I J K L M

tiptoe
to walk on your toes, trying not
to make a noise
I tiptoed past their room.

▲ tiptoe

trek
to walk a long way, especially
in hills or mountains
I'd like to trek in the Himalayas.

wade
to walk through water
I waded into the pond to get the ball.

wander
to walk without a purpose or
because you are lost
*They wandered in the forest for hours
before they found the camp.*

In other words

walk the plank (idiom)
to be forced to do something
This comes from the great age of sailing
ships, when someone who did something
wrong would have to walk out on a long
board (plank) and jump into the water.

N O P Q R S T U V W X Y Z

Want

aspire to
to want or hope to do something or be something, and work towards it
The story is about a girl who aspired to stardom.

crave

crave
to want something so much that you can't think about anything else
I woke up craving chocolate.

desire
to want something very much
You can have whatever you desire. There's something for everyone.

fancy
to want something
I fancy a walk, want to come?

hanker after
to think about something that you want but can't have
After a week at school, we were hankering after Mum's cooking.

hanker after

long for
to want something very much
We long for the summer holidays.

A B C D E F G H I J K L M

wish for

to want something to happen
I wish they'd hurry up and get here.

🌾 yearn for

yearn for

to want something so much that
you feel sad without it
The prisoner yearned for freedom.

a feeling of wanting something

impulse

a sudden feeling that you want
to do or have something without
thinking if it is a good idea
I bought this bag on impulse.

whim

a sudden feeling that you want
to do or have something
You can't get a puppy on a whim.

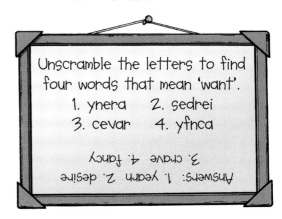

Unscramble the letters to find
four words that mean 'want'.
1. ynera   2. sedrei
3. cevar   4. yfhca

Answers: 1. yearn 2. desire
3. crave 4. fancy

Wet

clammy • damp • drenched • humid • moist

clammy
wet and sticky
When I'm nervous, the palms of my hands get clammy.

damp
slightly wet
These clothes are still damp from the rain.

drenched
extremely wet
The rain was so heavy we got absolutely drenched in no time.

moist
slightly wet
Keep the soil moist.

saturated
completely wet
The cloth is saturated, wring it out.

soaked
very wet
The cushions in the garden got soaked overnight.

 clammy

sodden
wet and heavy
The bottom of the box is sodden.

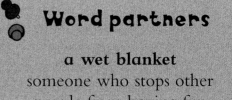

Word partners

a wet blanket
someone who stops other people from having fun
Look, I don't mean to be a wet blanket but turn the music down.

The opposite of
wet is dry.

waterlogged
so wet that something cannot hold
more water
*The pitch is waterlogged, so the match
is postponed.*

• **wet weather**

humid
wet and hot
It is hot and humid this time of year.

muggy
unpleasantly wet and warm
We don't like playing when it's muggy.

In other words

wet behind the ears (idiom)
young and inexperienced
*It's his first day working here.
He's a little wet behind the ears.*

Win

• a win

achievement
something that you
succeed in doing
*Setting a new school record
was an outstanding
achievement.*

conquest
a victory, usually if a
country takes control
of a place after winning
a battle
*The Norman Conquest was
led by William the Conqueror.*

In other words

**to win something
hands down** (idiom)
to win easily
Imogen won the race hands down!

The opposite of
win is lose.

landslide
when one side or candidate gets
many more votes than another
*The voting revealed that we had won
by a landslide.*

A B C D E F G H I J K L M

success
a win, especially in a series
of games, matches or fights
The match was our third success.

victory
a win, especially in a competition
or battle
*The streets were full of people celebrating
the victory.*

walkover
a very easy win, especially in sport
The set was a walkover for her.

• to win

sweep the board
to win all the points, medals or
prizes
*Our class swept the board at the sports
day competition.*

triumph
to win something
difficult or important
*It was a great triumph
for their team.*

win easily
to win a race or
game without
a lot of difficulty
*They won the first
few events quickly
and easily.*

walkover

N O P Q R S T U V W X Y Z

Work

drudgery • duties • grind • job • labour

labour
to work hard, usually doing something physical
The labour was long and hard.

push yourself
to force yourself to work hard
I had to push myself to finish.

push yourself

slave away
to work extremely hard at something that you do not enjoy
The sailors slaved away at the oars.

to be industrious
to work very hard and get lots of things done
You've been very industrious.

toil
to do boring work for a long time
In colonial times, thousands of people toiled in the plantations.

• **a task**

drudgery
work that is physically hard and boring
Working in factories can sometimes be drudgery.

duties
things that you have to do as part of your job
Everyone in the class has different duties.

grind
boring work
Memorising your times tables is a grind but it pays off.

grind

In other words

beaver away at (idiom)
to work very hard at something
He beavered away at his homework for hours.

This comes from the way beavers work when they build complicated dams.

job
the work that a person does to get money
Mum is looking for a new job.

Young

○ **a young person**

adolescent
a young person who is developing into an adult
Teenagers are adolescents.

infant
a baby or young child
I don't remember living there because I was an infant when we left.

◁ infant

juvenile
a young person
There are special rules for juveniles.

kid
a child
Don't be too hard on him – he's just a kid.

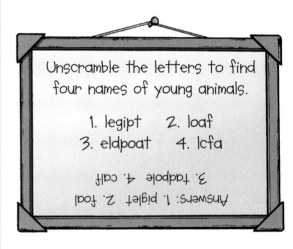

Unscramble the letters to find four names of young animals.

1. legipt   2. loaf
3. eldpoat   4. lcfa

Answers: 1. piglet 2. foal 3. tadpole 4. calf

minor
a legal term for a person who is not an adult
I'm afraid that minors must be accompanied by an adult.

A B C D E F G H I J K L M

• young

little

a sister or brother who is younger than you

My little brother is learning to walk.

small

The opposite of young is old.

Word partners

young at heart

to feel very young, even if you are not

I may be getting older, but I'm young at heart.

small

young, usually less than ten years of age

Dad says that when he was small, he couldn't swim.

Index

All the synonyms and their headwords in your book are listed alphabetically here. Simply look up the word you want to use – the headword for that entry is listed opposite in **bold** type.

Aa

Bb

backbreaking	see **Difficult**
baking	see **Hot**
balmy	see **Hot**
banal	see **Ordinary**
be aware of	see **Know**
be close to	see **Love**
be devoted to	see **Love**
be familiar with	see **Know**
be fond of	see **Love**
be well-up on	see **Know**
beam	see **Smile**
beat	see **Tired**
begin	see **Start**
behind someone's back	see **Secret**
benefit	see **Value**
bequeath	see **Give**
bicker	see **Argue**
big headed	see **Proud**
bit	see **Part**
blab	see **Talk**
bland	see **Ordinary**
blaring	see **Loud**
bluff	see **Pretend**
blunder	see **Mistake**
blurt out	see **Say**
boastful	see **Proud**
boiling	see **Hot**
bolt	see **Eat**
bolt	see **Run**

bona fide	see **Real**
bonus	see **Payment**
booming	see **Loud**
bound	see **Jump**
bowl	see **Throw**
brainy	see **Clever**
branch	see **Part**
brand name	see **Name**
break into a smile	see **Smile**
brand new	see **New**
bribe	see **Payment**
bright	see **Clever**
brilliant	see **Good**
bring	see **Carry**
brisk	see **Fast**
broke	see **Poor**
brood	see **Think**
buddy	see **Friend**
budge	see **Move**
build	see **Make**
burglar	see **Steal**
burgle	see **Steal**
burst out laughing	see **Laugh**

Cc

cackle	see **Laugh**
cagey	see **Secret**
can't bear/stand	see **Frightened**
carbon copy	see **Same**
care about	see **Love**
carry	see **Take**

cash	see **Money**	commonplace	see **Ordinary**
catch	see **Problem**	commute	see **Travel**
catnap	see **Sleep**	companion	see **Friend**
cease	see **Stop**	completely	see **Very**
central	see **Important**	complication	see **Problem**
challenging	see **Difficult**	component	see **Part**
change	see **Money**	comprehend	see **Understand**
character	see **Person**	concealed	see **Secret**
chat	see **Talk**	conceited	see **Proud**
cheerful	see **Happy**	conceive of	see **Imagine**
cherish	see **Love**	concoct	see **Make**
chew	see **Eat**	concrete	see **Real**
chilling	see **Frightened**	confidential	see **Secret**
chilly	see **Cold**	conquest	see **Win**
chore	see **Job**	consider	see **Think**
chortle	see **Laugh**	consistent	see **Same**
chuck	see **Throw**	consult	see **Ask**
chuckle	see **Laugh**	consume	see **Eat**
circle	see **Friend**	contemplate	see **Think**
clammy	see **Wet**	contempt	see **Hate**
clandestine	see **Secret**	content	see **Happy**
clash	see **Argue**	contrast with	see **Different**
close	see **Near**	converse	see **Talk**
clown	see **Funny**	convey	see **Take**
code name	see **Name**	cool	see **Cold**
coins	see **Money**	correct	see **Right**
comedian	see **Funny**	counterpart	see **Same**
comfortable	see **Rich**	covert	see **Secret**
comical	see **Funny**	crave	see **Want**
commence	see **Start**	create	see **Make**
comment	see **Say**	creep	see **Walk**

critical	see **Important**
cross	see **Angry**
crossing	see **Travel**
cross-section	see **Part**
crowd	see **Friend**
crucial	see **Important**
crumb	see **Part**
cry	see **Call**
cunning	see **Clever**
currency	see **Money**

Dd

daft	see **Stupid**
dainty	see **Small**
damp	see **Wet**
dash	see **Fast**
dash	see **Run**
daydream	see **Imagine**
deafening	see **Loud**
debate	see **Argue**
decent	see **Good**
decidedly	see **Very**
dejected	see **Sad**
delay	see **Wait**
delighted	see **Happy**
deliver	see **Promise**
deliver	see **Take**
demanding	see **Difficult**
demolish	see **Eat**
deposit	see **Payment**
deposit	see **Put**

depressed	see **Sad**
deprived	see **Poor**
desire	see **Want**
desolate	see **Sad**
despise	see **Hate**
despondent	see **Sad**
destitute	see **Poor**
detest	see **Hate**
devour	see **Eat**
difficulty	see **Problem**
digest	see **Understand**
dilemma	see **Problem**
dim	see **Stupid**
disadvantaged	see **Poor**
dispute	see **Argue**
dissimilar	see **Different**
distinctive	see **Different**
distribute	see **Give**
diverse	see **Different**
donate	see **Give**
doting	see **Love**
down	see **Sad**
doze	see **Sleep**
drain	see **Drink**
drained	see **Tired**
draughty	see **Cold**
dreadful	see **Bad**
dreading	see **Frightened**
dream of	see **Imagine**
drenched	see **Wet**
drift off	see **Sleep**

drop	see **Stop**
drop off	see **Sleep**
drowsy	see **Sleep**
drudgery	see **Work**
duplicate	see **Same**
duties	see **Work**
duty	see **Job**

Ee

ear-splitting	see **Loud**
ecstatic	see **Happy**
effortless	see **Easy**
elderly	see **Old**
element	see **Part**
embark on	see **Start**
end	see **Stop**
enquire	see **Ask**
epic	see **Story**
equivalent	see **Same**
errand	see **Job**
error	see **Mistake**
essential	see **Important**
establish	see **Start**
esteem	see **Value**
everyday	see **Ordinary**
examine	see **Look**
excellent	see **Good**
exclaim	see **Say**
excursion	see **Travel**

exhausted	see **Tired**
expert	see **Know**
explore	see **Travel**

Ff

fable	see **Story**
face lights up	see **Smile**
fake	see **Pretend**
false	see **Pretend**
family	see **Person**
fancy	see **Want**
fantasise	see **Imagine**
fantastic	see **Good**
fashion	see **Make**
fault	see **Mistake**
fed up	see **Sad**
fee	see **Payment**
feed	see **Eat**
feel	see **Know**
fetch	see **Carry**
fetch	see **Take**
feud	see **Argue**
fiddly	see **Difficult**
fight	see **Argue**
figure	see **Money**
fine	see **Payment**
finish	see **Stop**
fitting	see **Right**
flagging	see **Tired**
flee	see **Run**
fling	see **Throw**

flush	see **Rich**
folk	see **Person**
follow	see **Understand**
foolish	see **Stupid**
force	see **Open**
form	see **Make**
fortune	see **Money**
found	see **Start**
fraction	see **Part**
freezing	see **Cold**
fresh	see **New**
frosty	see **Cold**
fun	see **Good**
furious	see **Angry**
furtive	see **Secret**

Gg

gaffe	see **Mistake**
gag	see **Joke**
gallop	see **Run**
gang	see **Friend**
gaze	see **Look**
generate	see **Make**
genuine	see **Real**
geriatric	see **Old**
get	see **Understand**
ghastly	see **Bad**
giggle	see **Laugh**
give your word	see **Promise**
glad	see **Happy**

glance	see **Look**
glare	see **Look**
glimpse	see **Look**
glum	see **Sad**
go through with	see **Promise**
gobble	see **Eat**
goof	see **Mistake**
goosepimples	see **Cold**
gossip	see **Talk**
grasp	see **Understand**
great	see **Good**
grin	see **Smile**
grind	see **Work**
gruelling	see **Difficult**
guarantee	see **Promise**
guffaw	see **Laugh**
guide	see **Take**
gulp	see **Drink**
guzzle	see **Drink**

Hh

hair-raising	see **Frightened**
hallucinate	see **Imagine**
halt	see **Stop**
hand	see **Give**
handy	see **Near**
hanker after	see **Want**
hard	see **Difficult**
hassle	see **Problem**
haughty	see **Proud**
haul	see **Carry**

haunting	see **Remember**
heap	see **Put**
heartfelt	see **Real**
heave	see **Throw**
hero/heroine	see **Person**
hesitate	see **Wait**
hibernate	see **Sleep**
hiccup	see **Problem**
hidden	see **Secret**
high-speed	see **Fast**
highly	see **Very**
hike	see **Walk**
hilarious	see **Funny**
hindrance	see **Problem**
hint	see **Say**
historic	see **Important**
hold on	see **Wait**
homesick	see **Sad**
hop	see **Jump**
hopeless	see **Bad**
hospitable	see **Friend**
human/human being	see **Person**
humanity	see **Person**
humankind	see **Person**
humid	see **Wet**
humorous	see **Funny**
hurdle	see **Jump**
hurdle	see **Problem**
hurl	see **Throw**
hushed	see **Quiet**
hush-hush	see **Secret**

Ii

identical	see **Same**
identity	see **Name**
idiotic	see **Stupid**
idiot-proof	see **Easy**
impersonate	see **Pretend**
impossible	see **Difficult**
imposter	see **Pretend**
impoverished	see **Poor**
impressive	see **Good**
impulse	see **Want**
in jest	see **Joke**
in private	see **Secret**
in the vicinity	see **Near**
inaudible	see **Quiet**
income	see **Money**
incredible	see **Good**
incredible	see **Surprised**
indignant	see **Angry**
individual	see **Different**
individual	see **Person**
inept	see **Bad**
infant	see **Young**
inferior	see **Bad**
ingredient	see **Part**
initial	see **Name**
initiate	see **Start**
innovative	see **New**
insincere	see **Pretend**
inspect	see **Look**
instalment	see **Payment**

intellectual	see **Clever**
intelligent	see **Clever**
interrogate	see **Ask**
interview	see **Ask**
irate	see **Angry**
irritated	see **Angry**

Jj

job	see **Work**
jog	see **Run**
joking	see **Joke**
jolly	see **Happy**
journey	see **Travel**
joyful	see **Happy**
just	see **Right**
just out	see **New**
juvenile	see **Young**

Kk

key	see **Important**
kid	see **Young**
kidding	see **Joke**
kin	see **Person**
kip	see **Sleep**
kleptomaniac	see **Steal**
knowledgeable	see **Clever**

Ll

labour	see **Work**
landslide	see **Win**

lap up	see **Drink**
latest	see **New**
launch	see **Start**
lay	see **Put**
lead	see **Take**
lean	see **Put**
leap	see **Jump**
legend	see **Story**
lift	see **Carry**
light-hearted	see **Funny**
limp	see **Walk**
linger	see **Wait**
little	see **Small**
little	see **Young**
livid	see **Angry**
loathe	see **Hate**
lob	see **Throw**
local	see **Near**
long for	see **Want**
loot	see **Steal**
lope	see **Run**
lovely	see **Good**
low	see **Quiet**
low	see **Sad**
lug	see **Carry**
lukewarm	see **Hot**

Mm

mad	see **Angry**
maiden name	see **Name**
major	see **Important**

make sense of	see **Understand**	mumble	see **Say**
make-believe	see **Pretend**	munch	see **Eat**
manufacture	see **Make**	mundane	see **Ordinary**
march	see **Walk**	muted	see **Quiet**
marvellous	see **Good**	mutter	see **Say**
marvellous	see **Surprised**	myth	see **Story**
masquerade	see **Pretend**		
mate	see **Friend**	**Nn**	
meagre	see **Small**	name	see **Call**
meditate	see **Think**	namesake	see **Name**
memorable	see **Remember**	nap	see **Sleep**
mention	see **Say**	natter	see **Talk**
merit	see **Value**	naughty	see **Bad**
miniature	see **Small**	nearby	see **Near**
minor	see **Young**	needy	see **Poor**
minuscule	see **Small**	neighbouring	see **Near**
minute	see **Small**	neighbourly	see **Friend**
miserable	see **Sad**	neutral	see **Ordinary**
mischievious	see **Bad**	newcomer	see **New**
misjudge	see **Mistake**	next	see **Near**
mission	see **Job**	nibble	see **Eat**
mix-up	see **Mistake**	nice	see **Good**
modern	see **New**	nickname	see **Name**
moist	see **Wet**	noisy	see **Loud**
money	see **Money**	normal	see **Ordinary**
mould	see **Make**	not at all like	see **Different**
muffled	see **Quiet**	notable	see **Important**
mug	see **Steal**	noticeably	see **Very**
mugger	see **Steal**	novel	see **New**
muggy	see **Hot**	novel	see **Story**
muggy	see **Wet**		

Oo

occupation	see **Job**
open	see **Start**
original	see **New**
outing	see **Travel**
outstanding	see **Good**
overjoyed	see **Happy**
oversight	see **Mistake**

Pp

painless	see **Easy**
pal	see **Friend**
panic-stricken	see **Frightened**
particularly	see **Very**
pass	see **Throw**
pass on	see **Give**
passionate	see **Love**
pause	see **Stop**
pause	see **Wait**
peek	see **Look**
peep	see **Look**
peer	see **Look**
pelt	see **Throw**
pen name	see **Name**
penetrating	see **Loud**
penniless	see **Poor**
petrified	see **Loud**
phone	see **Call**
pick a lock	see **Open**
picture	see **Imagine**

piercing	see **Loud**
pile	see **Put**
pioneering	see **New**
place	see **Put**
plead	see **Ask**
pleased	see **Happy**
pledge	see **Promise**
poach	see **Steal**
pocket money	see **Money**
polish off	see **Drink**
poll	see **Ask**
pompous	see **Proud**
ponder	see **Think**
portion	see **Part**
pose	see **Pretend**
position	see **Put**
pounce	see **Jump**
practical joke	see **Joke**
prank	see **Joke**
precious	see **Value**
present	see **Give**
priceless	see **Value**
prise	see **Open**
prize	see **Value**
produce	see **Make**
profession	see **Job**
project	see **Job**
prompt	see **Remember**
prop	see **Put**
proper	see **Right**
prosperous	see **Rich**

pseudonym	see **Name**
pump	see **Ask**
pun	see **Joke**
punch line	see **Joke**
puny	see **Small**
push yourself	see **Work**

Qq

quarrel	see **Argue**
quench	see **Drink**
query	see **Ask**
question	see **Ask**
queue	see **Wait**
quick	see **Clever**
quick	see **Fast**
quickly	see **Fast**
quit	see **Stop**
quite	see **Very**
quiz	see **Ask**

Rr

rabbit	see **Talk**
race	see **Run**
rapid	see **Fast**
rate	see **Value**
realise	see **Know**
realise	see **Understand**
really	see **Very**
recall	see **Remember**
recent	see **New**

reckon	see **Think**
recollect	see **Remember**
reflect	see **Think**
refund	see **Payment**
regard	see **Think**
relive	see **Remember**
relocate	see **Move**
remark	see **Say**
remarkably	see **Very**
remind	see **Remember**
reminisce	see **Remember**
resentful	see **Angry**
retire	see **Stop**
reward	see **Give**
riddle	see **Joke**
ridiculous	see **Stupid**
ring	see **Call**
roar with laughter	see **Laugh**
roasting	see **Hot**
rob	see **Steal**
robber	see **Steal**
routine	see **Ordinary**
row	see **Argue**
rowdy	see **Loud**
rush	see **Fast**
rush	see **Run**

Ss

saga	see **Story**
salary	see **Payment**
saturated	see **Wet**

scalding	see **Hot**	sincere	see **Real**
scared	see **Frightened**	sip	see **Drink**
scary	see **Frightened**	skip	see **Jump**
scoff	see **Eat**	slave away	see **Work**
scream	see **Call**	sleepy	see **Sleep**
second-hand	see **Old**	sling	see **Throw**
section	see **Part**	slip	see **Give**
see	see **Imagine**	slip	see **Mistake**
see	see **Understand**	slumber	see **Sleep**
seething	see **Angry**	smarmy	see **Friend**
segment	see **Part**	smart	see **Clever**
sense	see **Know**	smirk	see **Smile**
set in motion	see **Start**	smug	see **Proud**
set up	see **Start**	snack	see **Eat**
share out	see **Give**	snag	see **Problem**
shattered	see **Tired**	sneer	see **Smile**
shepherd	see **Take**	snigger	see **Laugh**
shift	see **Move**	snobbish	see **Proud**
shivering	see **Cold**	snooze	see **Sleep**
shocked	see **Surprised**	soaked	see **Wet**
shoplift	see **Steal**	sociable	see **Friend**
shoplifter	see **Steal**	sodden	see **Wet**
shout	see **Call**	soft	see **Quiet**
shriek	see **Call**	solid	see **Real**
shrink	see **Small**	somebody	see **Person**
shrivel	see **Small**	someone	see **Person**
significant	see **Important**	spat	see **Argue**
silent	see **Quiet**	specialist	see **Know**
silly	see **Stupid**	speechless	see **Surprised**
simper	see **Smile**	speedy	see **Fast**
simple	see **Easy**	spicy	see **Hot**

spooky	see **Frightened**	support	see **Carry**
spot	see **Look**	surrounding	see **Near**
spring	see **Jump**	survey	see **Ask**
sprint	see **Run**	suspect	see **Think**
spy	see **Look**	swallow	see **Drink**
squabble	see **Argue**	swear	see **Promise**
squirm	see **Move**	sweep the board	see **Win**
stack	see **Put**	sweltering	see **Hot**
staggering	see **Surprised**	swig	see **Drink**
stall	see **Stop**	swing	see **Move**
stand	see **Put**	synonym	see **Same**
stand by	see **Promise**		
standard	see **Ordinary**	**Tt**	
stare	see **Look**	taciturn	see **Quiet**
stick to	see **Promise**	take	see **Carry**
still	see **Quiet**	taken aback	see **Surprised**
stir	see **Move**	tale	see **Story**
straightforward	see **Easy**	talented	see **Good**
streetwise	see **Clever**	task	see **Job**
strenuous	see **Difficult**	tear	see **Run**
stride	see **Walk**	tell	see **Say**
stroll	see **Walk**	tender	see **Love**
study	see **Look**	terrible	see **Bad**
stunning	see **Surprised**	terribly	see **Very**
subdued	see **Quiet**	terrified	see **Frightened**
success	see **Win**	the haves	see **Rich**
suitable	see **Right**	thick	see **Stupid**
sum	see **Money**	thief	see **Steal**
summon	see **Call**	thrilled	see **Happy**
superior	see **Proud**	thunderous	see **Loud**
supersonic	see **Fast**	tiff	see **Argue**

tiny	see **Small**
tip	see **Payment**
tiptoe	see **Walk**
tired out	see **Tired**
titter	see **Laugh**
to be getting on	see **Old**
to be industrious	see **Work**
toil	see **Work**
toss	see **Throw**
tote	see **Carry**
tough	see **Difficult**
tour	see **Travel**
trade	see **Job**
transfer	see **Move**
transport	see **Carry**
transport	see **Move**
transport	see **Take**
treasure	see **Value**
trek	see **Walk**
tricky	see **Difficult**
trip	see **Travel**
triumph	see **Win**
true	see **Real**
truly	see **Very**
typical	see **Ordinary**

Uu

unbolt	see **Open**
uncomplicated	see **Easy**
underprivileged	see **Poor**
undertake	see **Promise**

undertaking	see **Job**
unfold	see **Open**
unforgettable	see **Remember**
unhappy	see **Sad**
unique	see **Different**
unlock	see **Open**
unscrew	see **Open**
unwise	see **Stupid**
unwrap	see **Open**
used	see **Old**
useless	see **Bad**
user-friendly	see **Easy**

Vv

vain	see **Proud**
vary	see **Different**
vault	see **Jump**
verbatim	see **Same**
veteran	see **Old**
victory	see **Win**
vintage	see **Old**
visualise	see **Imagine**
vital	see **Important**
vocation	see **Job**
vow	see **Promise**
voyage	see **Travel**

Ww

wade	see **Walk**
waffle	see **Talk**

wages	see **Payment**
walkover	see **Win**
wander	see **Travel**
wander	see **Walk**
warm	see **Friend**
warm	see **Hot**
waterlogged	see **Wet**
wealth	see **Money**
wealthy	see **Rich**
weary	see **Tired**
weighty	see **Important**
well-heeled	see **Rich**
well-off	see **Rich**
whim	see **Want**
whisper	see **Say**
wide open	see **Open**
win easily	see **Win**
wisecrack	see **Joke**
wish for	see **Want**
within walking distance	see **Near**
witter	see **Talk**
witty	see **Funny**
wonder	see **Think**
wonderful	see **Good**
word for word	see **Same**
worn out	see **Tired**
worship	see **Love**
worth	see **Value**
wriggle	see **Move**
writhe	see **Move**

Yy

yarn	see **Story**
yearn for	see **Want**
yell	see **Call**